I0075003

Praise for
MANAGE SELF, LEAL
the book

All leadership is self-leadership first. My friend Nina makes it easy and effortless to master leadership and become exponentially successful.

Mark Victor Hansen
59 times #1 *New York Times* Bestseller

Nina's unique gift as a podcaster is her remarkable ability to create a space where guests feel truly seen and understood. Her thoughtful questions and genuine curiosity excavate insights about my leadership journey I hadn't fully articulated before. What sets her apart is how she combines warm generosity with incisive clarity, creating conversations revealing the authentic essence of her guests' experiences. I left our conversation feeling both energized and more deeply connected to my own leadership story.

Dan Silberberg
Thought Leader and Visionary, Entelechy.ai

Nina Sunday has brought together a collection of consummate thinkers, speakers, and pioneers; had deep delving conversations with them, then synthesised the collective wisdom into a uniquely practical, simply applicable set of tools for Leadership, with care and precision I've not seen before. Bravo Nina.

Allan Parker OAM
Microbehavioural Neuroscientist and Negotiator

Reading this book feels like being at the ultimate leadership dinner party—where the best guests show up, the conversation sparkles, and Nina keeps it all flowing with grace and brilliance. She's turned a podcast archive into a page-turner. Clever, curious, and quietly powerful.

Anneli Blundell
Author of *Developing Direct Reports*

This book is packed with gold for anyone serious about leadership. Nina has a rare talent for turning conversations into insight and insight into action. It's the kind of book that makes you think, and then do.

Chris Dyer
Author of *The Power of Company Culture*

The talented consultant, speaker and author, Nina Sunday has done it again. Her new book, *Manage Self, Lead Others*, draws its inspiration from her podcast. Readers will benefit from the wisdom of Thought Leaders on 10 different topics to assist their personal and professional development.

Pamela Wigglesworth
Communication Consultant, Experiential Hands-on Learning

What a read. Nina Sunday summarises what the best of the best in the world are saying about Self-leadership, Culture and Leadership. What a remarkable book! Forgive the mental image ... but crawl over broken glass to download this or have the book on your shelf. It's that good.

Ian Stephens
Triple Hall of Fame Award Winner, Speaker, Author and Trainer

Nina Sunday takes the heartbeat of her life's work and puts it into *Manage Self, Lead Others*, the book. More than leadership advice, it's wisdom, lived experience, and emotional intelligence from doing the real work. Being subtle, strong, and deeply human herself, Nina reveals extraordinary Joy Intelligence™. In every story, interview and insight, Nina draws the best out of her guests. To anyone who leads, listens and wants to do both with more purpose, this book is a gift.

Sheryl Lynn
Founder and Creator of JOYELY®, JOY Intelligence™

This book is a diamond mine! The ideas presented are clear, specific, and precise— and instantly useable. Everyone, from every walk of life, will find multiple takeaways for both their professions and personal lives. Read it!

Dr. Rich Allen
Educator and Master Trainer

The vast number of managers lack management skills and training to do their jobs, that is, to successfully hire, manage and exit, and within their relevant Employment Relations legislation framework. This negatively impacts productivity. Nina's book will help managers address this to build high performance teams.

Natasha Hawker
Author of *From Hire to Fire: Managing the Employee
Life Cycle—Hire, Manage, Wellbeing & Exit*

An amazing collection of valuable leadership insights from Nina and her podcast guests—all global thought leaders and high-performance practitioners. A must-read for all leaders who aspire to lead with impact and learn from the best.

Scott Dutton
Conflict Whisperer, fightingfair.com.au

MANAGE SELF, LEAD OTHERS^ε

Constructive Conversations,
True Self-Leadership
and Culture You Can't Fake

Nina Sunday

The National Library of Australia
Cataloguing-in-Publication entry:

Sunday, Nina

Manage Self, Lead Others: Constructive Conversations,
        True Self-Leadership and Culture You Can't Fake
ISBN: 978-0-9942353-7-4 (paperback)
ISBN: 978-0-9942353-8-1 (ebook, all formats)

1. General management. 2. Executive Management.
Title 658.4

BUSINESS & ECONOMICS
    Workplace Culture
    Mentoring & Coaching
    Skills

Interior design, cover design, and ebook formatting by Elizabeth Beeton

Other Works by Nina Sunday

Workplace Wisdom 9 to Thrive
978-0-9942353-2-9

Brainpower Smart Study: How to Study Effectively
978-0-9751941-5-7

Nina Sunday, CSP
BA (Eng / Psych), Dip Ed (Eng), Graduate of
Australian, Film, TV and Radio School 3-year
program

Curator of conversations, dolphin
swimmer and speed reading ninja

Award-winning Speaker for
conferences and workshops;
Founder Brainpower Training Pty
Ltd, Podcast Show Manage Self,
Lead Others, Author, C-Suite
Network Thought Council
Member

Dedicated to all my podcast guests.

Thank you for sharing your wisdom and stories.

You make the
Manage Self, Lead Others show
what it is.

CONTENTS

Nina Sunday

Nina Sunday

FOREWORD

Nina Sunday has done what most don't have the clarity or courage to do, taken years of conversations from her podcast with thought leaders, battle-tested entrepreneurs, and C-Suite veterans and distilled their wisdom into something actionable and powerful. This isn't theory; it's leadership in motion.

Nina gets it. Combining her own insights with candid input from some of the brightest minds in business, she turns it into something that actually works. Digging into the uncomfortable stuff—conflict, culture, feedback—she gives you a toolkit that's clear, sharp, and ready to use on Monday morning.

This book hits the sweet spot. It's smart, practical, and loaded with "why didn't I think of that" moments. Nina's voice is human and refreshingly direct.

This isn't a book you read and put on a shelf. It's a book you work with. You'll dog-ear the pages, highlight it, and come back to it when things get tough, because let's face it, real leadership is messy.

If you're ready to stop playing at leadership and start leading with intention, this is your playbook. Read it. Mark it up. Then get out there and lead like you mean it.

Jeffrey Hayzlett

PREFACE

The Pattern Beneath the Surface

During World War II, Alan Turing, the English mathematical prodigy with an IQ said to rival Einstein's, led the secret team at Bletchley Park that cracked the German Enigma code by designing the first thinking machine. After the war, Turing turned his attention from machines to biology and proposed something astonishing: that patterns in nature – like the stripes on a zebra or the spots on a leopard – could emerge from simple, repeated chemical signals.

This process, *morphogenesis*, reminds us that beneath the surface of what we see – in nature and in people – lie often hidden patterns shaping what unfolds. In teams, those patterns show up in the way we speak, avoid, listen, and react, especially when a conversation becomes awkward.

This book is about finding and working with those patterns. When you manage yourself first, you're better able to lead others through the conversations that matter most, the ones that shape trust, performance, and culture.

Turing wrote: *"It is suggested that a system of chemical substances, called morphogens, reacting together and diffusing through a tissue, is adequate to account for the main phenomena of morphogenesis."*

Leadership is similar – messy, chemical, unpredictable. But if you ignore the signals, you get patterns you never wanted: silence, blame, games people play.

Every time you set an expectation, give feedback, ask a question, or stay silent, you send a signal. And those signals don't disappear; they have a ripple effect. In a team, in a culture, across an organization, they begin to shape something recognizable: a pattern of performance, trust, accountability, or avoidance.

The conversations you have – or can't bring yourself to have – leave a trace. Over time, that trace becomes the culture. The question is: are you shaping it on purpose, or winging it and hoping for the best?

Workplace culture hides in plain sight. It doesn't live on posters or the CEO's pep talk. It lives in how we handle moments when things get real. Is yours flourishing – or just pretending?

It's time to change the language. Let's stop calling them 'Difficult Conversations.' When we label something difficult, we brace ourselves for tension, conflict, or awkwardness before we've even opened our mouths.

What if we flipped it? Let's start calling them Constructive Conversations – the kind that build clarity, trust, and real progress. Same issues, same truths, but a shift in mindset that makes all the difference.

You'll still see 'Difficult Conversations' in the podcast episode titles – because that's the language people use when they're searching for help. But inside this book, you'll learn to reframe them as Constructive Conversations. Same truths, less dread.

This book, *Manage Self, Lead Others*, is a pattern map.

Drawn from years of my conversations with thought leaders, experts, and changemakers on the *Manage Self, Lead Others* podcast, this volume distils the signals that matter most:

- Constructive conversations that create clarity

- Self-leadership that forms alignment

- Culture you can't fake

Whether you lead a team or just want to lead yourself better, this book gives you the tools to shape what others experience when they work with you. It will change how you see your workplace ... and the patterns that run it. And just as in morphogenesis, it starts with one small signal.

Then another.

Then another.

Until something real – maybe even beautiful – emerges.

INTRODUCTION

This isn't a book about a one-size-fits-all leadership model. It's a book about navigating the curveballs and fastballs of leading a team in today's VUCA world: volatile, uncertain, complex, ambiguous; especially in the age of AI.

The ideas inside are drawn from real conversations with some of the best business minds on the planet, featured on my podcast, *Manage Self, Lead Others*.

Content is also grounded in what I've seen firsthand, running hundreds of leadership and people skills workshops under the Brainpower Training banner.

This book blends evidence-based psychology, behavioural science and leadership lived experience. You'll find real case studies and big ideas, all designed to help leaders build cultures where people thrive.

My last book, *Workplace Wisdom for 9 to Thrive*, laid a foundation.

Workplace culture hides in plain sight. Is yours flourishing?

Why It Took Me Years to "Get" Leadership

If you ever found yourself leading a team for the first time and thought, *"What on earth do I do now?,"* welcome to the club.

The first thing they don't tell you? Leadership isn't about barking orders. It's also not about looking busy, spouting jargon, or pretending you know what's going on when you don't. It's about managing yourself first – your attitude, your ego, your ability to handle stress without turning into a dictator or a doormat.

Let's start with rookie mistakes. Every new manager makes them. Even seasoned pros still step in it now and then.

The first and biggest? Thinking you have to be the expert on everything. You don't. You won't be. And the more you pretend you do, the faster your credibility tanks.

Real leaders ask questions. They admit when they don't know. They surround themselves with people who do know, then get out of their way.

Then there's the "friend-to-boss" dilemma. One day, you're grabbing a wine with your coworkers, complaining about the boss; next day, you are the boss. Awkward!

If you think you can stay "one of the gang," think again. They're watching you now; how you handle pressure, how you react when things go south, whether you play favorites. You don't have to be a tyrant, but you do need to set a line – clear, firm, and nothing passive-aggressive.

Let's talk about meetings. If not handled well, it can be a graveyard for productivity. If your calendar is packed with pointless meetings, congratulations. You've officially become part of the problem. Meetings should be short, sharp, and with a purpose. If people walk out thinking, *That could have been an email*," you failed.

This isn't about playing boss. It's about leading. Keeping your team engaged, getting results without turning into a micromanaging control freak, and, let's be honest, making sure you maintain your sanity in the process.

The road to being a great leader is paved with trial, error, and the occasional disaster. But if you manage yourself first, you're already ahead of the curve.

A Hard Lesson in Leadership

I wasn't always a leader. In fact, I wasn't even trying to be one. Before I built a 7-figure business, before I hired a single person, I was just another cog in the corporate machine; showing up, doing my job, and waiting for someone, anyone, to notice that maybe I had more to offer.

But no one did.

Back then, leadership wasn't something people talked about. You weren't mentored, guided, or even nudged toward growth. You were hired to do a job, and that was it.

No one cared about my career progression, my potential, or whether I could be something more. When the reality set in, that I wasn't going to climb any corporate ladder, I stopped looking for the next rung and started looking for the exit.

I built my own ladder.

Self-employment was a natural move. I had ideas, I had ambition, and most importantly, I was done waiting to be found. And here's the thing – when you step into leadership without a playbook, you tend to do what was done to you. And what was done to me? Nothing.

I hired people, I set targets, I pushed for results. I thought culture was just a side dish, something you sprinkled on top with a few team outings and birthday cakes in the break room.

And then I couldn't help but notice my business started bleeding talent.

At first, I chalked it up to bad hires. But the pattern was undeniable. New employees would come in fired up, then plateau, then spiral downwards.

Some quit. Others stayed, but their negativity was like a slow leak in the hull of a ship. It dragged everything down. And I – fearless, self-made entrepreneur that I was – had no clue as to why.

Then it hit me. Culture isn't a side dish. It's the whole meal.

While I spent years obsessed with numbers, productivity and hitting targets, I ignored the thing that actually made those results sustainable; the workplace environment I was creating.

When I finally got it, when I started putting culture first, everything shifted.

People stayed. They worked harder, not because they had to, but because they wanted to. The business thrived. And I finally learned what leadership actually was.

My First Scar

The realization didn't come out of nowhere. A coach asked me this question, *"What is your first scar in business?"*

When I looked back over my past work history, a moment came to mind; one I hadn't thought about in years. A moment that had quietly shaped the way I avoided confrontation and leadership for far too long.

I was 20, studying at university, working part-time for a company that ran speed reading courses including free introductory sales presentations. They sent me to a small town about 90 minutes' drive away from the metropolitan city where we usually did our promotional talks using TV and radio advertising.

This time, the situation was one of those rare, perfect storms. Local TV and radio ads ran for a free presentation in a local hall. What we didn't factor was that this small town had been in the TV viewing zone of the nearest metropolitan city. For a year, they'd seen our ads for presentations in the big city. Now, we were finally on their doorstep.

Setting up in the hall expecting the usual 30 – 50 people, at 5 minutes before start time, with no warning, our little venue was suddenly swamped with a packed house; 80 people crammed into a small hall with standing room only at the back.

It was the kind of moment where you sink or swim, and I swam. I adjusted on the fly, kept the energy up, and somehow, pulled it off. At 20 years of age, I had just spoken to 80 people, nailed the presentation, and got a goodly number from a room full of strangers to sign up for a course.

I walked into the office next morning, expecting a pat on the back. Instead, my boss glared at me, stony-faced, looking like someone had served him cold coffee.

I sat down at his desk all smiles. But his face was like a storm cloud. In an angry whisper, he seethed, *"You lost me money!"*

I blinked. What the … ?

I'd just pulled off something huge, and this boss was telling me I wrecked it.

"Don't you know … you should put a 'Full House' sign on the door as soon as all the chairs are taken! You don't just let everyone in. Standing-room-only loses money."

I sat there stunned. I'd done everything right – adapted, performed, made it work. And yet, in his eyes, I had failed.

I didn't know how to answer. I quickly left fighting back tears. A week later, I quit.

At the time I didn't connect the dots. Years later I realized what that moment had done to me. It wounded me, and I still carried the scar. It led me to believe that performance feedback wasn't about growth; it was about blame. And that belief shaped how, decades later, I abdicated leading my own team.

When I started hiring people, I avoided one-on-one coaching conversations. When people justified, denied, or made excuses for their behaviour, I didn't think on my feet; instead I floundered.

If someone's behavior was dragging the team down, I'd grit my teeth and tolerate it, hoping it would fix itself. Part of me thought, if I call someone out, they will get upset then decide to leave, just like I did all those years ago.

And the truth? The real truth? I didn't know exactly what to say or how to say it.

Then one day I read something – probably an article, maybe a book – and it clicked. There is a formula for these conversations; a way to give feedback without destroying morale, a way to lead.

So, I tried it.

And it worked.

What I had feared for years, that coaching someone would make them quit, wasn't true at all. People didn't leave. They improved. They appreciated the clarity, the directness. And suddenly, I saw leadership for what it really was: not just driving results, but creating a workplace environment where people wanted to be.

At the end of the day, results aren't the goal, culture is. Get that right, and the numbers take care of themselves.

Rookie Leader Mistake: Thinking Group Meetings Are Enough

A couple of decades ago, I landed a government grant to develop a business plan, (something I'd never done before).

The process involved bringing in a business planner to conduct a 360-degree feedback assessment; a fancy way of saying, let's find out what your team really thinks of working with you.

Up until that point, I thought I had a solid grip on team communication. We had meetings, we discussed business goals, we tackled challenges together. Everyone had a voice, or so I thought.

Then the business planner sat me down and said something that stopped me cold.

"Your people haven't told you this, but this is what they told me."

And there it was. The blind spot I hadn't seen.

I had assumed that holding group meetings meant we were having real conversations. But in reality, I had never created a space for one-on-one dialogue. There was no private, direct line of communication where someone could say, *"Nina, I'm struggling with this,"* or *"Here's what's getting in the way of my work."*

Instead, the only option they had was to bring up concerns in front of the whole team. And let's be honest, who's going to risk looking like the only complainer in a room full of colleagues?

So they stayed silent. They buried their frustrations. And when the business planner asked them, one-on-one, what was stopping them from doing their best work, they told him everything.

And I never saw it coming.

Why One-on-Ones Matter More Than You Think

That experience hit me hard. I had been so focused on big-picture strategy and team discussions that I completely missed the personal, human side of leadership.

When I finally reflected on it, I realized something simple but game-changing:

People don't just want to be heard. They want to be heard in a space where they feel safe enough to be honest.

That's what one-on-ones create. A private, open conversation where someone can say:

- Here's what's blocking me from doing my best work.

- Here's what I need more clarity on.

- Here's what's frustrating me about how we work.

And when you, as a leader, actually listen, when your team knows you have their back, that you'll help remove obstacles, it builds something no group meeting ever could: loyalty, trust, and real connection.

Without that, people start venting elsewhere. And that's the silent killer of team effectiveness.

When people feel unheard, resentment festers. They don't complain to you; they complain about you. They whisper in hallways, roll their eyes in meetings, and slowly, without you even realizing it, they disengage.

That's why one-on-ones aren't optional. They're not a nice-to-have, and they're definitely not the same thing as a formal performance appraisal (which, let's be honest, most people dread).

They're the conversations that stop problems before they start.

The Question That Changed How I Lead

After that wake-up call, I started asking myself a different question:

"What would I want people to do for me if I were in their role?"

Or even better, *"What did former bosses NOT do for me that I wish they had?"*

For me, the answer was clear. I wished someone had taken the time to meet with me, not as part of a group conversation, but with the respect and attention of a one-on-one meeting, to ask privately with genuine interest:

"What's making your job harder than it needs to be? What can I do to help?"

That's when I understood: leadership isn't just about guiding the team. It's about clearing the path for each of them.

That was one thing I was not doing. And once I fixed it, everything changed.

So, if you're leading a team, ask yourself, *"Are you giving people the space to tell you what they really need? Or are you just assuming they'll speak up in a meeting?"*

That's a rookie, new manager mistake. And it's one I won't make again.

The Power of One-on-Ones.
How a 20-Minute Conversation Changed Everything

Years after that first hard lesson in leadership, I had a simple one-on-one with a Client Liaison team member in our conference room. Nothing formal, just a conversation.

A staple tool in any training company is the flipchart, so I grabbed a marker and sketched out 2 columns:

"Like to do" vs. "Not my preference"

"Let's list all the tasks you do," I suggested. *"Then you rate them as either "Like to do" or "Not my preference."*

At first, it felt routine. Just a way to map out responsibilities. But as we went down the list, I noticed something surprising. A couple of regular, everyday tasks landed in the *Not my preference* column.

And that's when it hit me.

How would I have ever known this if I hadn't asked? She wasn't unhappy. She wasn't complaining. She was simply carrying out tasks she tolerated but didn't enjoy.

And here's the surprising part:

Some people on our team actually liked doing those exact things.

So, I asked, *"You know, we've got Katrina and Maggie. What if I see if one of them wants to swap a task with you?"*

She loved the idea. We set up a task rotation, and just like that, we gave everyone a broader workplace experience.

Delegation, Done Right

That moment made me rethink how I approached delegation.

A quality question from Priority Management is:

"Who else can do this?"

For years, I held on to certain tasks because I felt they were too important to hand off. Case in point: workshop confirmations.

This was a high-stakes admin task. One small mistake in pricing could cost us hundreds of dollars. I was convinced that only I could do it properly.

Then I gazed across the open-plan office towards one of our team members. She handled our client follow-ups. I remembered she previously worked as Qantas ground crew.

I took a chance.

"I know you were in ground operations before. Did that involve admin work?"

She nodded. *"Yeah, a lot."*

Boom! There it was. She was already experienced with high-detail, high-stakes tasks. Why hadn't I asked sooner?

"Four-Eyes" Control: A simple fix that saves hours

To make the handover work, we put a simple control mechanism in place:

The Four-Eyes Control Principle:

> 2 people to check every confirmation document
> before sending.

She prepared it. I reviewed it.

That one shift saved me countless hours, and we've used Four-Eyes Control ever since.

One-on-Ones: The 20-Minute Leadership Tool that Changes Everything

That's the thing about making time for one-on-ones. They don't have to be long. But they create clarity, connection, and efficiency.

In just 20 minutes, I:

- Learned what tasks drained the life out of my team members
- Discovered who actually became energized by those same tasks
- Freed up my own time by delegating smarter
- Helped people grow in ways I hadn't realized they wanted to

And it all ties back to the error of thinking leadership is about knowing everything. The reality? It's about knowing your people. And the easiest way to do that?

Ask.

Rookie Mistake: Believing Leadership Is About Having All the Answers

Early on, I thought being a leader meant I had to know everything.

Not in an ego-driven, *"I'm the smartest person in the room"* kind of way, but more the *"I need to prove I belong in this role"* kind of way.

I had built the business, hired the team, and now I figured, it was up to me to have the solutions. If there is a problem, I have to fix it. If someone needs guidance, I am to provide it. If something isn't working, the answer has to come from me.

I didn't see it at the time, but this mindset, this need to prove my own credibility, was quietly closing off innovation, shutting down fresh ideas, and keeping my team from stepping up.

Here's how I went from *"I Have to Solve Everything"* to *"Let's Figure This Out Together."*

I stumbled across a Harvard Business Review case study on Project Oxygen, a research initiative by Google's People Lab that studied what makes a great manager. They identified 8 essential leadership behaviors.

And guess what?

Technical competence, the very thing I was leaning on, was dead last.

At the top? Helping people with career progression. Creating a positive culture. Understanding what's going on in people's lives.

That was a gut check. I was so focused on being technically competent that I had missed the bigger picture of what leadership actually meant.

So, I started making some changes.

17

Using Personality Insights
to Work Smarter, Not Harder

One shift I made was introducing psychometric assessments; not to box people in or label them, but to understand how they naturally worked.

I love using the DiSC® profile because it reveals patterns; not just in how people think, but in how they execute tasks. Once I started looking at how my team naturally approached work, I could stop pushing square pegs into round holes.

I could delegate smarter, match people with tasks they'd thrive in, and encourage innovation instead of shutting it down.

A Simple Change that Transformed Team Culture

Around the same time, I read about a company that introduced group morning tea; a structured break where people sat together for a few minutes each day instead of grabbing their coffee and retreating back to their desks.

I thought, *"Why not?"*

So we started gathering 3 days a week around 11 AM – nothing rigid, just a quick coffee or tea together for 15 minutes.

And here's what I didn't expect ... this small change completely reshaped our team culture.

In those casual conversations, I found out:

- Who had an ill parent they were caring for

- Whose child was about to sit their final exams

- Who was planning an overseas trip they were excited about

The fun, the struggles, the real stuff.

It changed how we worked together. People weren't just colleagues; they actually cared about each other. And when people care, they collaborate better, they support each other, and they enjoy coming to work.

Culture wasn't something I had to force anymore; it was taking care of itself.

Keeping It Productive: The "Mini-Meeting" Trick

Of course, there was a balance to strike. Morning tea could have easily spiralled into a half-hour chat session, which wouldn't have worked for productivity.

So, I introduced a simple transition cue.

After 15 minutes, I'd announce: *"Mini meeting!"*

We'd spend a further 5 minutes discussing a quick business update, then people would head back to their workstations.

It was a win-win:

- We maintained social connection.

- We made time for informal problem-solving (those "water cooler moments" companies used to rely on).

- It kept our productivity on track.

What I Learned

I look back now and realize how easy it is for leaders to fall into the "I have to know everything" trap.

But the truth is, leadership isn't about proving yourself. It's about helping your team shine.

- It's about asking instead of assuming.

- It's about creating a culture where people feel valued.

- It's about realizing that the best ideas often come from your team, not from you.

Once I made that shift, I stopped worrying about whether I was qualified enough to lead. Plus, I started enjoying my team more than ever.

Phubbing at Morning Tea:
How I Handled a Subtle Culture Clash

After we introduced the regular group morning tea, a new team member joined in. Well ... sort of.

While the rest of us chatted, he leaned back in his chair, eyes glued to his phone, scrolling away as if the conversation around him didn't exist.

It wasn't outright rude, but it was off.

Here we were, fostering team connection, sharing stories, throwing around ideas, and he was checked out, lost in his own digital world.

I recognized this was one of those defining leadership moments. Ignore it, and phone-scrolling would become the unspoken norm. Call it out in front of everyone, and I'd just embarrass him. Neither option felt right.

So, I took the middle path – a private conversation.

Later that day, I pulled him aside and explained the history of our morning tea tradition.

"For years, everyone just grabbed their own coffee and went back to their desk. We barely talked. Then I introduced group morning tea; not as a meeting, but as a way to connect. A time to share a little about life outside of work, swap ideas, and sometimes, yes, problem-solve on the fly."

I made it clear:

- Stopping for morning tea wasn't mandatory, but it was about face-to-face interaction.

- It wasn't about productivity; it was about team culture.

- There were plenty of other times to check your phone. Morning tea just wasn't one of them.

He got the message. The next day? No phone. He joined the conversation. Phubbing (phone snubbing) stopped.

Why This Matters More Than You Think

On paper, morning tea is not a meeting. But in reality? It functions like one. When done regularly it builds things leaders want in a team:

- *Trust* – because people feel heard.

- *Positive communication* – because conversation is part of the routine.

- *Team spirit* – because connection isn't forced; it happens naturally.

- *Approachability* – because leadership feels human, not distant.

- *Recognition* – because small wins get celebrated.

Birthdays, engagements, new homes, new babies ... these moments might not seem like "work" conversations, yet they're the glue that holds a team together.

And the best part?

You don't have to *create* a positive team culture, you just have to *make space* for it to happen.

That's what morning tea does.

Rookie Mistake:
Not Finding the Right Words Until It's Too Late

Early in my leadership journey, I was what you might call an avoidant manager.

I wasn't big on confrontation, so I let small behaviors slide, convincing myself it wasn't a big deal. Pick your battles, right? Until those small behaviors stack up like dirty dishes in a kitchen sink. Suddenly, you've got a mess no one wants to deal with.

The problem? Those small behaviors weren't isolated moments, they were patterns. And I had one team member whose pattern I couldn't ignore.

The Behavior I Couldn't Unsee

At the time, I had an office with a glass wall overlooking 5 open-plan workstations. From my desk, I could see almost everything.

And I started noticing something odd.

Every time I walked out of my office, one particular team member would spring back into her chair, as if I'd caught her doing something she wasn't supposed to.

At first, I brushed it off. People chat at work. It's normal. But this wasn't once or twice. It was constant. She wasn't just chatting; she was interrupting herself and the person in front of her.

I knew I needed to address it. But I hesitated.

What do I say? How do I bring this up without sounding petty?

I convinced myself that saying something would be micro-managing. That I couldn't tell people not to talk at work. That it would just make things awkward.

So I did what a lot of rookie managers do.

I said nothing.

The Conversation I Should Have Had

Looking back, I now know exactly how I should have handled it.

I could have pulled her aside and said something simple.

"I notice when I walk out of my office, you quickly stop talking and spring back into your chair. It looks a bit like a guilty reaction. Are you feeling uneasy about something?"

No accusations. No drama. Just curiosity.

Because that's leadership … asking, not assuming.

But instead, I avoided the conversation altogether. And the problem didn't go away.

Finding My Voice (A Little Too Late)

Over the summer I read Eli Goldratt's *The Choice*, a book that shifted how I saw leadership.

Goldratt, a physicist-turned-management-guru, was famous for his Theory of Constraints, the idea that every system has a major bottleneck, and if you fix that, everything else automatically improves.

And what did I realize? The biggest constraint in my business at that moment was me. More specifically, my silence.

Goldratt had another philosophy – any disharmony reduces profitability. And there I was, constrained by awkward silence and unresolved tension, all because I hadn't found the right words to cut through the noise.

I finally had the conversation.

It turned out, she had originally been hired as an appointment setter. But the business had evolved in the last 3 years, and I didn't need to be so busy running around seeing clients in their workplace anymore.

We had to decide, could we create a new role for her, or would she prefer to find a different opportunity that's a better fit for her skills?

When she eventually left, it was the right move for both of us. A few months later, I was asked to give her a reference – for an Executive Assistant role.

That told me everything. She had been underutilized in my company, and that was demotivating for her. She needed a nudge in the right direction and leaving my small business was better for her. We restructured to incorporate temporary gap year students (between high school and university, or after university before finding a corporate role).

Find Your Voice Before It's Too Late

I look back now and realize:

- I was too slow to address the obvious.

- After 3 years, she needed a fresh opportunity to re-motivate.

- My small business simply didn't have the scope to provide that.

And none of it would have dragged on if I had just found my voice sooner.

That's the mistake of not learning how to say what needs to be said, in the right way, at the right time.

And that's what I call a "never again" lesson.

Episode 118:
Rookie Mistakes
New Leaders Make

Nina Sunday with Brendan Rogers

Rookie Mistakes New Managers Make

It's Not Just About the Numbers

Becoming a leader isn't just about hitting numbers and executing strategies. It's about building people. I was a guest on Brendan Rogers' *Culture of Leadership* podcast, which I later re-published on *Manage Self, Lead Others*. Brendan's questions explored the nuanced, messy, human stuff most new leaders overlook.

Focusing on the Work, Not the People

One classic blunder? Ignoring your core responsibility: creating new leaders. Early in my career, I was so caught up in proving I had the answers that I missed the bigger picture. You're not just managing a team; you're shaping future careers. The minute I realized my role is to nurture growth, engagement got a boost. People stuck around longer, even in a small business where career paths may seem limited.

Delegating without Strategy

Then there's delegation and job rotation, tasks leaders too often mishandle. Delegating isn't just offloading work. It's understanding strengths. I learned this the hard way when a straightforward task ballooned into a 4-day research marathon because I'd handed it to someone who valued precision over brevity. Understanding your team's behavior preferences whether through DiSC® or other tools, lets you delegate smarter. You save time, reduce stress, and build deeper capability.

Shutting Down Innovation

Let's talk about innovation. Early in my leadership journey, I was guilty of accidentally shutting down new ideas prematurely. It felt easier to reject suggestions from the sidelines rather than invite dialogue. That is a rookie mistake. Embracing Kaizen, the philosophy of continuous improvement, helped me flip that script. Good ideas often lead to great ones if you just give them room to breathe.

Neglecting Informal Culture

There's also power in informal culture-building rituals. Simple practices like shared morning teas or regular casual catch-ups can be transformative. They're not time-wasters; they're connectors. When people genuinely know each other, productivity and loyalty flourish. (Just watch out for smartphones stealing these precious moments. Set boundaries clearly.)

Dodging the Tough Conversations

Finally, language matters. Early on, I avoided confronting minor issues, thinking they'd resolve themselves. They don't. Conversations addressing behavior don't have to be confrontational.

The simple Scott Dutton approach, *"I noticed ... and I don't know if you're aware of that"* (see next chapter) often works wonders without bruising egos. I learned that leading from the front – clear, direct, and respectful – beats issuing instructions from the sidelines every single time.

Progress Over Perfection

Leadership isn't about perfection. It's about learning, growing, and owning your mistakes. So go ahead, make them, but don't repeat them.

CONSTRUCTIVE CONVERSATIONS

We might have named this chapter "Performance Conversations."
But the moment we name it "Constructive Conversations,"
we unlock something bigger:
not just a measure, but a signal for growth.

The Art of Giving Feedback:
2 Paths, 2 Styles

I've spent a lot of time thinking about feedback. Giving it, receiving it, getting it wrong, getting it right.

Reflection is what separates amateurs from professionals. The more I explore, the more I realize there isn't just one way to do it.

Early on I latched onto a method: BFIR; a structured, no-nonsense approach:

1. Behavior
2. Feeling
3. Impact
4. Request

It gave me a template of exactly what to say, *It's direct, it's clear, and it gets results.*

But I have to remember TIMTOWTDI – there is more than one way to do it.

One Way to Give Feedback

Ever tried to give feedback at work, only to watch the atmosphere get awkward real fast? Or maybe you swallowed saying what you think, afraid that whatever comes out will backfire?

Let's be real. Calling out poor behavior is an art. Do it wrong, and you've got an argument on your hands. Do it right, and you might, perhaps, get through to someone. The key? Don't wing it. Be intentional. Choose your words like a pro.

When I first set out to improve the way I gave feedback, I knew I needed a structure, something to keep me from either over-explaining or going in too soft. That's when I found this formula, BFIR.

It gave me just enough of a framework to be clear, direct, and still keep things professional. So, I started using it. And to my surprise, it worked. Not perfectly every time, but better than the freewheeling approach I'd been taking before.

But feedback is an evolving process, and I wasn't done learning. I kept experimenting, kept testing different ways to get through to people. And eventually, I found another method; one that took feedback to the next level. We'll get to that soon.

For now, here's the first tool I found and put to work.

BFIR Feedback Formula

B—Behaviour
(start with the facts)

"When you ... "

(Describe exactly what happened. Stick to what you saw, not what you think they meant.)

F—Feeling
(make it personal, but not a blame game)

"I feel / I felt ... "

(Use real emotions: frustrated, disappointed, annoyed. Not *"you made me feel,"* because that's a guaranteed fight-starter.)

I—Impact
(why this actually matters)

"Because what happens is ... "

(Explain the ripple effect. Maybe it cost time, money, or patience. Make it real.)

R—Request
(what you want instead)

"And what I'd like to see in future is ... "
   (Be clear. No passive-aggressive hints. Just say what needs
   to change.)

The Finisher

End with a question:
   "What are your thoughts?" or
   "Would you be willing to do this?"

This keeps it a conversation, not a lecture.

Example in Action

1. *When you ...* (showed up late to the meeting)

2. *I felt ...* (annoyed)

3. *Because ...* (impact; we wasted time going over
    things everyone else already heard)

4. And what I'd like to see in *future* is ... (you
    showing up on time.)

    What are your thoughts?

This isn't just for negative feedback. It works just as well when
someone nails it. Flip the last step to reinforce great work:

Positive Example

1. *When you ...* prepped the meeting so well

2. *I felt ...* of your effort

3. *Because ...* the client signed off on our proposal
    in 5 minutes

    I look forward to seeing ... more of that in the
    future.

The Bottom Line

Feedback isn't about making someone feel bad. It's about making things better. Use this technique at work, at home, with friends, family, even your barista if they keep getting your order wrong. The more you practice, the easier it gets.

Quick Pro Tips

- Rehearse before using it live. You don't want to sound hesitant or blurt out a word that triggers a poor response.

- Give feedback often. Don't save it for the annual review.

- Ditch using "always" or "never." They start fights, not solutions.

- Say "I felt," not "you made me feel." One is your truth. The other is an accusation.

- Don't assume intent. Stick to what happened, not why you think it happened.

At first, I thought this was the best way to give feedback. And for a while, it was. But then, I stumbled onto another approach; one that shakes up everything I thought I knew. We'll get to that next.

Upon reflection, while some situations call for blunt force, others need something finer, something more precise. I started wondering if there were a better way.

Could feedback be just as effective without it feeling like a confrontation?

That's when my podcast, *Manage Self, Lead Others*, led me to a conversation with mediator, Scott Dutton.

Episode 86:
Difficult Conversations

Scott Dutton

In Search of the Perfect
Constructive Conversation Method

I thought I had feedback figured out.

BFIR was my go-to method; a structured, no-nonsense approach getting straight to the point.

That's when my podcast, *Manage Self, Lead Others* led me to Scott.

While some situations call for blunt force, others need something finer, something more precise.

Could feedback be just as effective without feeling like it's a confrontation?

Scott is a different breed of feedback guru. Where I saw precision and clarity as the holy grail, he saw conversation, emotion, and relational dynamics as key.

His approach is softer, more fluid. Less about delivering a verdict, more about drawing people into dialogue.

If BFIR is a finely honed chef's knife, Scott's method is more like slow braising; letting flavors develop, tension ease, and truth emerge naturally.

His technique reframes issues in neutral terms, so when the conversation begins, defensiveness isn't already in play.

Scott tells me, *"I say, 'Hey, if you've got a few moments, I'm just wondering if we could have a chat about meeting times and see if we're on the same page.'"*

I start by asking for their input first: *"I just want to get some clarity on what time you're thinking we start,* or *"how you're finding meetings are going."*

They might say, *"I'm all good with meetings."*

Then I'll gently bring it up: *"Look, I'm not sure if you're aware, but when you're not coming at 9, it often delays a meeting getting started while we're waiting for you, and that impacts our ability to get through the agenda. And I'm not sure if you're aware of that."*

Scott explaining this method of bringing up the subject got me asking myself, what kind of leader do I want to be? One who delivers the cleanest, sharpest feedback possible, or someone who makes space for conversation, coaxing people toward their own realization?

The reality is, both approaches work. But timing is everything. Sometimes you need the precision of BFIR; other times, the relational intelligence of Scott's style. The real skill is knowing when to use which.

I joked with Scott, *"Your method is like tickling with a feather, while I've been swinging a sledgehammer."*

He smiled and nodded. *"Some people may need a sledgehammer,"* he confided, *"but most don't."*

That stuck with me.

Episode 136:
Difficult Conversations

Lisa McInnes-Smith

And that brings me to my conversation with Lisa McInnes-Smith.

If Scott Dutton is about softening the edges of feedback, Lisa is about lighting people up from the inside. She doesn't just talk about leadership; she embodies it, breathing energy into every room she enters. If there ever is a lesson in how presence and passion shape leadership, Lisa is it.

Lisa's take? Conflict avoidance is leadership avoidance. Leaders who dodge constructive conversations aren't protecting team harmony. They're letting dysfunction fester.

And the biggest mistake? Thinking one conversation will fix it. Conflict resolution isn't a one-and-done deal; it's a process; a slow, deliberate recalibration of habits and expectations.

She drives home a key point. Trust isn't automatic, it's built. And the fastest way to destroy it? Ignoring problems, pretending they don't exist, or letting resentment quietly build. Trust isn't just about transparency. It's about having the courage to address issues before they spiral.

And when you do address them? Set the conversation up to win. Don't ambush. Don't turn it into a courtroom cross-examination. Set the tone, choose the environment, even take it outside for a walk if needed. Key is keeping the conversation productive, not punitive.

And the truth is, most people aren't being difficult on purpose. They're reacting either to unclear expectations, or poor communication, or a work environment where they don't feel valued. Lisa emphasized curiosity over assumption. Before jumping to conclusions, leaders need to ask better questions.

So here's the throughline. Feedback isn't just about fixing what's broken. It's about creating momentum, shaping culture, and calling people to something greater.

Whether you take the precision route, the conversational route, or the full-throttle inspiration route, the goal is the same, to help people do better what they already do well.

And that's the work. That's the craft. That's leadership.

Episode 137:
Crucial Conversations

Andrew Bryant

Leadership is a Conversation

When it comes to constructive conversations, Andrew Bryant doesn't shy away from hard truths. One of the most profound takeaways from our discussion is this: if someone can't receive feedback, that itself becomes a feedback issue.

In Andrew's words, *"Then we have to have a crucial conversation; feedback on their ability to take feedback."* That's when leadership steps into its grittiest terrain – confronting behaviour that hasn't changed, even after agreements were made. And not with blame or shame, but with clarity and conviction: *"If these behaviours continue, they are not tenable with everybody."*

It's this kind of courage that separates surface-level management from true leadership. Performance isn't just about setting goals and measuring results. It's about setting the tone for accountability, and having the tough conversations when people fall short.

Andrew explains that leadership is, at its core, a conversation. And often, problems arise not because someone failed to act, but because someone failed to speak. A leader's silence can become the unintentional permission slip for poor behaviour. That's why, as he puts it, *"leadership is the worst behaviour a leader will tolerate."* If someone's late to meetings and it goes unaddressed, that lateness becomes the new normal.

He also introduces a vivid metaphor: the fish under the table. Unspoken issues rot over time. But if you *"put the fish on the table,"* you can address it, cook it, deal with it. Left hidden, it stinks. So constructive conversations, no matter how awkward, are essential to maintaining trust, accountability, and momentum.

For Andrew, decisiveness isn't about dominating. It's about creating clarity. It's setting expectations, following through, and making sure that when feedback is given, it's not just heard, it's acted on. That, he says, is what performance leadership really looks like.

Episode 124:
Unmasking Leadership

Dan Silberberg

The Power of Curiosity

But my journey wasn't over. The emotional precision of managing conversations was richer and more complex than I'd ever imagined. And I was determined to keep digging.

Scott Dutton softens the edges, Lisa McInnes-Smith ignites passion, Andrew Bryant clarifies the stakes, next Dan Silberberg reminds us of the subtle art of conversational curiosity. I knew I was onto something special.

"I'm curious."

Two simple words yet packed with possibility.

In one of his many episodes as a repeat guest on my podcast, *Manage Self, Lead Others*, Dan Silberberg reminds us of the value of using this opener phrase to start a question.

"I'm curious" opens doors without kicking them down. It invites honesty without defensiveness. It isn't accusatory; it's exploring. It positions the leader not as the interrogator, but as someone genuinely interested in understanding the other's perspective first.

Could the key to great feedback really be this simple? Could starting a question with *"I'm curious"* bridge the gap between clarity and connection?

Dan was creating psychological safety, an environment where ideas could flow without judgment.

"If you want innovation," Dan explained, *"then you need vulnerability and a psychologically safe environment allows for*

people to say, 'I'm not sure about that idea,' or 'I've tried something similar before, got some great results, and here's what I learned.' There's openness."

And then he says it, the phrase that immediately clicks for me:

"I'm curious ... if we were to do this, what outcomes do we expect?"

"I'm curious ... why do you think this idea will leverage the best results?"

It was brilliant. *"I'm curious"* isn't just about ideas. It's about tone, intention and openness.

It strips away defensiveness and invites dialogue. It's light but purposeful, neutral but engaging. It positions the leader not as judge or jury but as genuinely interested, ready to explore possibilities.

As I listened, I realized something important; innovation and constructive conversations aren't so different. Both require an openness to uncertainty, a willingness to hear perspectives that might differ radically from our own.

"I'm curious" could be the bridge I was looking for between clear communication and emotional intelligence.

Episode 147:
Performance Conversations

Bruce Sullivan

2 Agreements Method

Bruce Sullivan emphasizes 2 agreements. First, start with intention.

"Hey, my intention is to have a healthy working relationship with you. And my intention is to have a conversation with you that takes us closer to that. I have a couple of things to talk to you about that hopefully helps us get closer to that. Can we have that conversation now? Have I got your permission?"

Bruce explains that if you get permission at that point, you already have the first agreement. It's not just about a behavior, it's about the intention and the impact.

Another way to ask, *"Do we both agree we're going to keep this conversation healthy and constructive and positive, working towards having a healthy working relationship?"*

If they ask, *"Well, what is it?,"* I go back to *"I don't want to talk about what it is until we both agree we're going to be as constructive and as helpful and as mindful as we can. So can we work towards this really good working relationship?"*

With those agreements in place, it's easier … but there's no guarantee. If it goes out of shape with responses like, *"You're just picking on me,"* or *"This is unfair,"* go back to the intention, *"What I want is a conversation about making this a really great place to work and better understanding about our part in that. So can we please come back to that, if that's OK?"*

Only after gaining these agreements do you introduce the actual issue. It's not a confrontation; it's a collaborative conversation.

Bruce's Two Agreements Method shifts the weight from personal criticism to shared goals.

Suddenly the conversation isn't about blame; it's about building something better together. Then the next question to ask, *"Ok. Well, when [this] comes up, what do you think the impact is on some people when this behaviour presents?"*

This means he is not talking about the behaviour. He's talking about the impact of the behavior.

And now here's where Bruce demonstrates he's mastered conversation elegance. If at any point they reply, *"I don't know,"* Bruce responds with, *"If you can imagine that you did know, what would the answer be?"*

Bruce has his conversation toolkit ready with responses to add to in the moment. It really does make a difference.

Episode 153:
HR: From Hire to Fire

Natasha Hawker

Directness with Respect

Then I meet Natasha Hawker, a Human Resources expert who pulls no punches. Natasha's style is refreshingly direct and clear. For her, constructive conversations only become difficult when leaders avoid them.

"Normalize feedback," Natasha emphasizes. *"Tell your team upfront, 'I'll regularly give feedback about what's working and what's not, so that it won't feel personal or unexpected.'"*

She recommends daily "huddles" – short, regular touchpoints that build a rhythm of transparency. Frequent check-ins become normal, expected, and safe.

But Natasha also stresses vulnerability. *"Be honest when feedback might be hard to hear. Say it upfront, 'I'm going to share something you might not want to hear, but I believe it'll help you grow.'"*

If you think it'll hurt, acknowledge that. *"This might be uncomfortable."* Let them respond, because even their reaction tells you something valuable.

Highlighting the power of genuine listening, Natasha elaborates, *"It's important to let people express their feelings; especially if they're defensive or upset."*

Acknowledge what they're feeling. "It seems like I've upset you. It seems like you're angry. Can we talk about what's happening here?"

She believes regular check-ins, even daily huddles, build trust, reduce anxiety and prevent misunderstandings from escalating into full-blown conflicts.

And Natasha raised another important angle, the exit conversation.

"Conduct exit conversations with someone neutral; not their boss. People leaving the business have nothing to lose, so they'll be honest. Use those insights to improve."

She even suggests the proactive approach of "stay conversations," i.e. identifying flight risks early to retain valuable team members.

Could curiosity, paired with Bruce's structured agreements and Natasha's direct yet respectful approach, finally solve the puzzle of constructive conversations? I was eager to test it further.

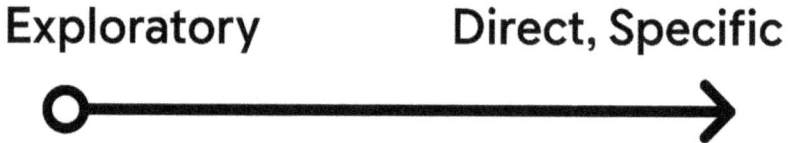

Exploratory   Direct, Specific

Looking back across my conversations, I begin to see a continuum emerging:

1. **BFIR Method:** Direct, structured, specific
   Behavior, Feeling, Impact, Request
   Getting straight to the heart of the issue.

2. **Scott Dutton:** Neutral, gentle invitations, such as
   "I don't know if you're aware of that ..."
   encouraging awareness without defensiveness.

3. **Lisa McInnes-Smith:** Clear differentiation between acceptable and unacceptable behavior, emphasizing finding courage to directly address issues.

4. **Dan Silberberg:** Genuine curiosity, starting conversations with *"I'm curious ..."* to foster openness and exploration.

5. **Andrew Bryant:** The directness of *"putting the fish on the table,"* i.e. openly addressing issues before they fester.

6. **Bruce Sullivan:** Two Agreements Method, agreeing on the intention before mentioning the impact of a specific behavior. This conversation isn't about blame. It's about building something better together.

7. **Natasha Hawker:** Normalizing feedback with regular dialogue. Directness combined with respect and vulnerability, and upfront acknowledgment of the potential difficulty of the conversation.

Each of these approaches has its place. Together, they offer a powerful toolkit to transform difficult conversations from dreaded encounters into opportunities for genuine growth and stronger relationships.

I was getting closer to mastering the art of ***constructive*** conversations. Perhaps I'd finally found the range, the continuum, I was searching for.

Table 1: Continuum of Effective Feedback

OPEN AND EXPLORATORY $\longrightarrow$ **CLEAR AND DIRECT**
(SOFT) — **(FIRM)**

2. **Scott Dutton:**
   "I'm not sure if you're aware ... " (invitational, gentle)

1. **Nina Sunday:**
   BFIR (structured clarity, straight to the point)

3. **Lisa McInnes-Smith:**
   Acceptable vs. unacceptable behaviors

4. **Andrew Bryant:**
   "Put the fish on the table" (direct, addresses unacceptable behavior head-on)

5. **Dan Silberberg:**
   "I'm curious ... " (open, exploratory)

7. **Natasha Hawker:**
   Direct, respectful, upfront honesty

6. **Bruce Sullivan:**
   Two Agreements (collaborative, goal-oriented)

In this continuum:

The **LEFT** side emphasizes a softer approach, openness, curiosity, and collaborative exploration.

The **RIGHT** side emphasizes clarity, directness, structured confrontation of specific behaviors, and setting clear boundaries.

Episode 56:
Leadability

Rowdy McLean

Then there is Rowdy McLean.

If Natasha Hawker delivered directness wrapped in vulnerability, Rowdy took it a step further. He didn't just prefer honesty, he insisted on fast feedback.

"Performance reviews every 6 months or yearly?" Rowdy shook his head. *"That's ridiculous. If Nina looks disengaged or unmotivated, I want to talk about it now, not 6 months from now!"*

For Rowdy, the holy grail is immediacy, dealing with things when they happen, in real-time. And to pull that off, he had his own stripped-down approach, the 60-Second Method.

He wasn't into long-winded setups or elaborate formalities. Instead, he kept things lean, direct and observant.

Here's how it goes:

Start by stating exactly what you observed – no drama, no blame, just plain, neutral facts. *"I just saw the customer leave looking pretty unhappy. Can you tell me what happened?"*

No blame, no judgment, just an observation, leaving space for the other person to fill in the blanks.

That simple technique – observation, then curiosity – opened the door wide enough for honesty, without kicking it down. And here's the magic: more often than not, people willingly step through that door themselves.

Rowdy nailed it with an example: Maybe the person tells you straight up, *"Yeah, look, my bad. The kids kept me awake last night, the dog ran away, and I'm burned out."* Well, now we're talking – literally. We're on the same side. Now we can actually do something productive.

But what's even more powerful about Rowdy's method is the subtle but crucial distinction he draws between observing and blaming. It's the difference between *"Why were you rude to that customer?"* and *"I noticed the customer didn't seem very happy. Any reason?"* The first demands defense, the second invites reflection.

As Rowdy points out, going into conversations swinging blame rarely achieves much, other than maybe a flash of defensive adrenaline and a quick descent into stalemate territory. Observing, on the other hand, makes room for real dialogue, real solutions.

Suddenly, it makes sense. This isn't about being soft vs. tough. It's now about timing, tact and tone. It's about knowing when to turn up the heat, when to dial it down, always starting from curiosity and clarity rather than accusation.

I had over 100 podcast episodes, each with another perspective, another tool, another angle. What I'd initially imagined as a tidy, one-size-fits-all formula had transformed into something far more powerful – a continuum, sliding effortlessly between curiosity and directness, from exploratory openness to the clean, cold light of clarity.

The beauty is in the nuance; the flexibility to move along this scale depending on the situation, the person, and the stakes.

That felt real. That felt human. And frankly, that felt like leadership.

Episode 77:
Developing Direct Reports

Anneli Blundell

I was looking for an answer; a clean, one-size-fits-all method. And the deeper I went, the clearer it became: constructive conversations weren't about absolutes, they are about choices along a sliding scale of clarity, curiosity, and courage.

I had more than 160 podcast episodes, with experts weighing in on what to say, do and be. Let's continue the exploration and see where it leads.

Which brings me to my conversation with Anneli Blundell.

Anneli literally wrote the book on it, *Developing Direct Reports*. Her take was refreshing, direct, and stripped of pretension. It wasn't long before we got straight to the heart of what she calls "leadership derailers."

She hit me with a surprising fact, one that felt both validating and surprising.

"The most common leadership derailer? Conflict avoidance," she said. *"Leaders who dodge tough conversations, hoping the issue resolves itself. It never does. It festers."*

Turns out, my past aversion to confronting small behaviors wasn't unique; far from it. According to Anneli, conflict avoidance was tied for number one among the 12 leadership derailers she identified in her research. In short, avoiding tough conversations was practically universal!

She dropped a comforting bombshell: I wasn't alone.

"Nearly half of people would rather quit their job than face a difficult conversation," she explained. *"It's in our DNA. We're wired to seek belonging, to avoid rocking the boat. Conflict triggers ancient alarms in our brain. It feels like social danger."*

Anneli laid it out straight. Leaders struggle with conversations because they blow them out of proportion. *"We make a difficult conversation harder than it need be by amplifying its importance in our head,"* she said. Her solution was practical and grounded. *"Imagine treating difficult conversations as regular conversations. The only difference? You prepare your words. You know what to say, you set the tone, and then you simply speak."*

I recognized myself in that. How often had I agonized over confronting a minor issue, twisting myself into knots, only to discover afterwards that clarity and courage would have kept it simple?

Anneli pushed even further into practicality.

"You don't develop people through annual performance reviews alone," she said. *"That's ridiculous. Growth happens every day, in small moments, through small conversations. It happens when you pay attention, when you're prepared to ask, to coach, to gently challenge."*

She emphasized building capability through targeted stretch opportunities. Find real projects and tasks that align with someone's growth goals. *"And confidence?"* Anneli added. *"If someone feels 100% ready, it's too late; 40% ready is enough. That's where real growth lives."*

There was something distinctly refreshing about Anneli's frankness. Forget perfection, forget waiting until you feel completely ready. Growth happens when you dive in, uncertain but willing.

She even nailed the specific language leaders could use to take the edge off: *"I'm going to share something that might be hard to hear, but I genuinely believe it'll help you grow."* This wasn't sugarcoating. It was respectful honesty. Sometimes being blunt was a kindness.

As Anneli laid out her thinking, it all clicked into place. My search for a cheat sheet had evolved into something richer. Something more adaptable. Something more powerful. The holy grail wasn't a script; it was a continuum, flexible enough to handle the nuances of human behavior, clear enough to guide action.

I'd spent years searching for the right template, a single perfect approach. But conversations weren't cookie-cutter affairs. They were fluid, nuanced, and shaped by context.

And suddenly, the idea of leadership was coming into sharp focus. You couldn't lead without conversation. You couldn't grow people without connection. And you couldn't connect without courageously stepping into discomfort, embracing the moment, and simply starting to speak.

That was the craft.

That was the work.

And frankly, that felt real.

Episode 131:
The Power of Company Culture

Chris Dyer

Then there is Chris Dyer.

Chris has a refreshingly different angle, zeroing in on how organizations handle mistakes; not just feedback, but genuine human missteps. Mistakes are inevitable, but how leaders respond? That's a choice, and it shapes the entire culture.

Chris made a critical distinction upfront:

"Errors are when someone isn't paying attention, hasn't been properly trained, or is multitasking. That's sloppy. We don't accept that.

Mistakes happen when someone genuinely tries something new. They use the information they have at hand, make a decision, and then later realize, 'Hey, that didn't pan out as I expected.'

How leaders handle these moments can either fuel growth or crush initiative. It's a sliding-door moment. Do you educate or punish?

Chris used the example of Southwest Airlines, famous for their relaxed cabin announcements; "loosey-goosey," as he put it.

Southwest's secret? They created a culture where mistakes weren't career-ending events. Public blunders became teachable moments behind closed doors. Employees weren't humiliated or reprimanded in public; they were supported, retrained, and sent back out wiser, better prepared.

"They're not afraid to have fun because they know, if they step out of line, they're not fired on the spot," Chris explained. *"They're guided, supported, coached. That's how you build psychological safety."*

It clicked immediately. This wasn't just about mistakes. It was about trust. A culture of blame makes people risk-averse. But a culture that treats honest mistakes as moments for growth empowers everyone to show up, to speak out, and to innovate without fear.

Chris reinforced the theme I'd been exploring from multiple angles. Effective leadership hinges on knowing exactly what to say and how to say it when things inevitably go off-script.

It was another piece of the puzzle. Conversations weren't just about correcting behavior. They shaped the fabric of teams, creating the invisible rules that either energized people or drained them.

Suddenly, it all came together ... the sliding scale, the nuanced continuum from curiosity to specificity, from openness to directness, and now another critical insight; how you respond to human error shapes your culture, your leadership and your legacy.

Leadership isn't about perfection. It's about how you handle imperfection.

It felt good to finally see it clearly.

Episode 74:
Difficult Conversations Made Easy

David Deane-Spread

David Deane-Spread, a former Australian Defence Force officer and covert ops leader turned corporate CEO … if anyone knew something about courage under pressure, it was him.

David didn't mince words. When I asked about the biggest mistake leaders make with difficult conversations, his answer was starkly simple:

"Fear."

"The biggest mistake is not dealing with the issue because they're too afraid," David said plainly. *"They put their head in the sand, avoid it, or pretend it'll magically disappear."*

I recognized myself immediately. Not dealing with something minor, letting it fester until restructuring the entire business felt easier than facing one uncomfortable conversation. Turns out, I wasn't alone. David had seen this scenario plenty of times before.

"Leaders often think restructuring is easier than facing someone who's particularly skilled at fielding, or causing, difficult situations," he explained. *"But that's just kicking the can down the road. The hard conversation doesn't vanish. It festers, multiplies, infects."*

His solution wasn't complex, but it was profound. David created a straightforward method and named it **OLART**:

- **Observe and Listen**: Pay attention without judgment. Take in what's happening visually, audibly, emotionally.

- **Listen more than you Ask,
  Ask more than you Tell,
  and Rarely Tell.**

It's a simple hierarchy. Listen deeply. Ask meaningful questions. Only tell if absolutely necessary, and even then, sparingly.

David illustrated with striking clarity how this played out in practice.

Instead of confronting someone with *"You're rude to customers,"* he suggested saying calmly, *"Help me understand what's happening. You seem upset. Is there something going on that I should know?"* And critically, he added another key question: *"What do you think we could do about it?"*

That approach was powerful for 2 reasons. First, it diffused defensiveness immediately by inviting explanation rather than blame. Second, by asking the other person for solutions, it placed accountability squarely back with them; exactly where it belongs.

But David also nailed the subtler details, the physical choreography of the conversation:

"Never have these conversations in front of others," he stressed. *"Sit or walk side-by-side rather than face-to-face. It burns off anxiety chemicals. Go outside. Take a walk."*

It reminded me instantly of a moment I'd forgotten; training with Nigel Paine, former Head of BBC Learning, who used "walk-and-talk" conversations, around the block, to bring out insights that never emerged sitting around a table. I'd forgotten how powerful the simple act of walking and talking, side-by-side could be.

David's method resonated because it was deceptively simple, yet deeply human. Observe carefully, listen openly, ask before you tell, invite the other person's solutions, and then keep the conversation moving, literally and figuratively.

It felt right. It felt human.

This wasn't a quick-fix template. It was a roadmap, clear but flexible enough for the messy reality of human emotions.

Constructive conversations are no longer something to avoid; they are the daily work, the necessary craft, the essence of leadership. And finally, they are starting to feel achievable, perhaps even natural.

Episode 115:
Executive Lion Taming

Carol Marzouk
The Executive Lion Tamer®

Some guests enter my podcast gently, offering subtle insights. Then there was Carol Marzouk, who arrived like a force of nature, earning her moniker as the Executive Lion Tamer® from a bold act of fearless confrontation.

Carol specializes in taming executives' challenging behavior, the kind whose aggressive personalities can tear teams apart – or even bring down a company. She has the kind of job most people would avoid like the plague – confronting leaders who see themselves as untouchable rainmakers, often oblivious to their own destructiveness.

Carol didn't waste time making her point.

She opened with a story about a high-performing lawyer, an alpha rainmaker, whose personal mantra might as well be, *"It's everyone else's job to adapt to me."*

At the request of a managing partner Carol lunched with him. The conversation began predictably enough, with the lawyer confidently explaining, *"I don't need fixing. I bring in all the money. It's everyone else who needs to adjust."*

Carol, not one to indulge ego, gave him her card anyway, fully expecting it to end up tossed into the nearest trash can.

It didn't.

A month later, Carol received a call from this lawyer. His voice was tense, defensive and on edge. *"I threw a chair at an associate,"* he confessed bluntly. *"It didn't really hit her, just grazed her shoulder. But now there's a lawsuit. I am coachable. Please come fix this."*

Carol, unfazed, dryly asked, *"Are you calling me because you need better aim?"*

Humor didn't land well with him, but the moment was pivotal. It wasn't the lawsuit itself that had finally humbled him, but the dawning realization that he'd crossed a line. As Carol explains, these types often remain blind to their toxicity until they hit rock bottom; like addicts finally forced into confronting their destructive behaviors.

She pointed out a truth that resonated deeply: *"It's never really about skill; it's about will. Most people are coachable, but not until the stakes are high enough."*

Carol's method begins with a crucial understanding: people are icebergs. What you see above the surface – their abrasive comments, arrogant posturing, passive-aggressive snipes – is only a small fraction of what's really going on. The true motivations, insecurities, and pain lie hidden beneath the waterline.

"The trick," Carol explained, *"is to get beneath the surface in a non-invasive way. To understand what really drives them, their emotional currency, you don't get there through confrontation. You get there through curiosity."*

Curiosity; there it was again; Dan Silberberg's *"I'm curious"* resurfacing, proving that constructive conversations are less about confrontation and more about understanding.

According to Carol, the mistake leaders make is believing these abrasive personalities can't or won't change. *"98% are surprisingly coachable,"* she insisted. *"They just need someone willing to see past the bravado to the insecurity beneath."*

She outlined 3 distinct types of aggression – verbal and physical aggression (like the chair-thrower), active aggression (cutting remarks, overt hostility), and the insidious passive-aggression. *"Passive-aggression,"* Carol warned, *"is often the hardest to spot, like nodding in agreement but walking out the door backward. It's subtle, corrosive, and leaves the team confused and on edge."*

Then there's outright bullying. Carol emphasized a startling observation from her thirty-year career: *"Every bully I've encountered, no matter how successful or powerful, is fundamentally insecure. Power doesn't erase insecurity; often, it amplifies it."*

It reminded me sharply of my own experience managing a team, when one employee's passive-aggressive tone undermined not just my authority but the morale of everyone around her. It felt petty at first to confront, but Carol made clear it was anything but petty. Ignored, such toxicity multiplies, infecting the entire team.

Carol's strategy was nuanced but strikingly practical:

> **First**, recognize toxic behavior as pain. *"People can't give what they don't have,"* Carol explained. *"If someone isn't kind, they're lacking kindness inside. Their aggression is a cry for help, whether they know it or not."*

> **Second**, she emphasized grace, offering understanding before correction. *"The worse they behave, the deeper their pain. Meet aggression with compassion first."*

Then, crucially, introduce accountability, not blame. *"We're all enablers of toxic behavior when we ignore it,"* Carol said bluntly. *"The solution? A clear, consistent system where accountability becomes normal. Everyone is working on something. No one is singled out."*

Her process, refined through years of trial and error, unfolds in 3 powerful stages:

- **Detox:** Self-awareness first. Understand your own biases, fears, and triggers before confronting others.

- **Engage:** Earn the right to lead. Actively listen, *"listen with a pen,"* she suggests. Write it down, reflect it back, and truly hear what others have to say.

- **Unite:** Build a culture where trust isn't a buzzword but an everyday reality. *"Design your culture intentionally, then live it."*

Carol was clear-eyed about the necessity of regular one-on-ones. *"Take them out of the office, for a walk, for coffee. Conversations about careers, motivators, demotivators. It's never too late. You've never waited too long to show genuine care."*

She drove the point home with a powerful example: an employee on the verge of leaving was offered triple the pay elsewhere. But she stayed, not because of money, but because her manager finally "knew her," her motivations, her frustrations, her humanity.

"Never underestimate how powerful it is to simply see your people as whole humans, not just workers," Carol said. *"When you unite a team by truly understanding each other, loyalty becomes almost unbreakable."*

As she spoke, I understood something clearly. What I'd been searching for wasn't just a conversation cheat sheet or the perfect feedback method. It was the deeper art of truly knowing people; the iceberg beneath the surface.

Carol, the Executive Lion Tamer®, had laid bare a profound truth. Taming lions wasn't about force or coercion. It was about compassion, curiosity and courage. And maybe that's exactly the point of leadership itself.

From "Shame on Me" to "What Brings You Joy?"

Carol Marzouk nailed it when she told me, *"It's never too late."* She gave me the perfect opener to a conversation I'd been avoiding, even after decades of working side by side with someone. *"You know, shame on me for not asking sooner,"* she says, disarming in her honesty. *"But I've been thinking about how important you are to me. Where do you see yourself in a year?"*

59

Simple. Human. Real.

Yet many leaders never ask, convinced they've missed the boat. But as Carol showed, vulnerability goes a long way in softening old resentments and reopening doors long assumed shut.

Episode 12:
Empathetic Conversations

Dr Rich Allen

Dr Rich learned a technique in his early twenties that has stayed with him ever since. A simple, powerful way to hold truly empathetic conversations.

The Common Mistake

Most people, Dr Rich says, want to be empathetic. But when someone shares something emotionally significant, many listeners instinctively jump in with reassurance: *"You'll be fine. Don't worry about it."*

It seems kind, but it shuts the conversation down.

The Muck of Missteps

Dr Rich and I demonstrated some of the common traps, the "muck" that derails conversations when someone shares emotional content.

1. Reassurance

Nina says: *"Dr Rich, I'm having problems with my flatmate at the moment."*

Dr Rich says: *"Nina, you are always in control of things. This doesn't sound like a big deal. You will be fine."*

The problem? As Dr Rich points out, they have not even listened to the problem yet.

2. Identification

Nina: *"Dr Rich, I'm having problems with my flatmate. I do not know what to do."*

Dr Rich: *"I know just what you mean. I had a nightmare flatmate once too."*

Suddenly, the spotlight shifts from the speaker to the listener. Dr Rich explains, *"When someone is sharing emotionally, you have to keep the spotlight on them."*

3. Irrelevant Questions

Nina: *"Dr Rich, I am having real problems with my flatmate."*

Dr Rich: *"Oh, what is her name? When did she move in? How big is the house?"*

Asking situational questions misses the point. Emotional issues need emotional space, not trivia.

4. Hijacking

Nina: *"Dr Rich, I'm having problems with my flatmate."*

Dr Rich: *"You think that is bad? My boss is a nightmare."*

Again, the speaker gets pushed aside. Dr Rich notes, *"It is fine in casual conversations, but when someone shares deeply, you have to know when to step off that habit."*

5. Lecturing

Nina: *"Dr Rich, I'm having problems with my flatmate."*

Dr Rich: *"You know, Nina, you do this a lot. You get into tussles over unimportant things. Maybe you should look at yourself."*

It insults rather than helps. *"Managers sometimes do this without realising,"* Dr Rich adds. *"It shuts people down."*

The Real Work: Listening Without Fixing

Dr Rich stresses the importance of holding space when someone shares emotionally.

Instead of trying to reassure, hijack, or fix, the best response is: *"Sounds like that is really important to you. Tell me more."*

Let the person talk. Let them descend the "ladder" of conversation until they reach their real bottom line, the true heart of their issue.

What About Giving Advice?

Dr Rich warns against giving direct advice.

If they ignore it, they feel guilty.

If it fails, they blame you.

If it succeeds, they may become dependent on you for every decision.

Episode 121:
Career Questions to Ask

Brian Bowman

Career Questions

Which brought me to an exploration from my podcast archives, a conversation with Brian Bowman, a straight-talking, thoughtful expert in career development who offered concrete, actionable ways to turn overdue career chats into transformational moments.

Brian, a learning strategist I'd collaborated with years before, knew exactly why managers freeze when it comes to career conversations. *"We're great at tactical coaching, the everyday stuff. But lift us out of that daily grind into a discussion about someone's future, and we often stumble."*

For Brian, career conversations aren't about scripting someone's future for them. Instead, they're about igniting a spark, helping someone realize what brings them joy, where their passions lie, and how those passions align with their work. His questions weren't the usual corporate-speak platitudes; they were real, tangible, and surprisingly human.

"What brings you joy?" Brian asked me rhetorically, knowing the power of that simple question. It wasn't a soft, fluffy sentiment. It was targeted insight, a way to uncover what really energizes someone. *"When are you in flow? What are you naturally drawn to throughout the day?"*

As Brian spoke, I could see it clearly; employees lighting up when they finally connect what they love doing with what their job can offer. It wasn't about endless training modules or checklists. It was about recognizing patterns, watching where their enthusiasm naturally landed and helping them chase more of it.

He pushed further, asking questions most leaders forget, or fear, to ask:

"What would you love to do at work that you're not doing right now?"

It was a deceptively powerful question. Suddenly, employees aren't just clocking hours; they're dreaming, plotting, imagining what could be. They see themselves contributing in new ways. It's permission to admit ambition without guilt or fear.

Brian warned against the classic trap leaders fall into, focusing exclusively on skill-building, courses, microlearning, and neglecting real-world experiences. *"Skills matter, sure,"* Brian conceded, *"but experience is king. Managers have to intentionally craft opportunities for their people, moments where they're challenged, stretched, and exposed to new situations. It's those moments, not certificates, that truly advance a career."*

The old concept of linear careers, climbing a predictable corporate ladder, is fading fast, Brian noted. He loved the phrase "squiggly careers," paths shaped by sideways moves, unexpected leaps, detours into seemingly unrelated roles. These squiggles aren't setbacks. They're rich experiences that fuel growth. *"Those skills,"* he emphasized, *"are transferable. Always."*

Brian's conversation touched something essential. He described a common rhythm in careers, the classic 3-year cycle. The first year is mastery – learning, adapting. The second year, excelling, really owning the role. But by the third year, restlessness sets in. Employees look up, look around, and ask, *"What's next?"*

"It's exactly then," Brian said, *"that leaders have to engage, long before boredom sets in."* He referenced management thinker Charles Handy and his concept of the sigmoid curve, the insight that motivation peaks, then wanes unless leaders intervene proactively. *"If you wait until motivation dips, you're already too late."*

His point was sharp. When managers hoard their best talent out of fear of losing them, they ironically hasten their departure. *"We think keeping people means hiding opportunities, hoping they never see greener grass. But the opposite's true. The more openly you invest in their growth – even if it means you're preparing them for a future beyond your team – the more loyalty you inspire."*

This resonated deeply. Good leadership isn't squeezing every ounce of productivity. It's about a duty of care. Brian put it beautifully. *"Your role as a leader is to ensure their CV is always marketable. A great employer prepares people for their next job, even if it's not with them."*

Brian highlighted how Simon Sinek describes younger employees demanding rapid progression without experiencing real adversity. *"Sinek compares it to sailing through a storm. You might do the same tasks as someone experienced, but have you weathered a storm? Have you proven you can handle crisis?"* It was another stark reminder that experience – messy, real-world lived experience – is irreplaceable.

Brian Bowman had clarified something essential. Career conversations aren't something to dread. They're your greatest tool for inspiring loyalty, commitment, and genuine growth. And as Carol reminded us, no matter how long overdue, it's never too late to start the conversation.

With Carol's raw vulnerability and Brian's practical clarity, the roadmap for meaningful career conversations became crystal clear – human, real, vulnerable, and powerful.

No more excuses. Time to talk.

Episode 43:
Strategic Leadership

Val Grubb

Carol Marzouk got the ball rolling. It's never too late to ask. Brian Bowman followed with the right questions to unlock career direction. Now, Val Grubb took it a step further: don't just help people grow; help them think big.

Her message was clear and unapologetic. If your employee wants to be CEO, help them get there.

That kind of leadership scares some managers. They hear "CEO" and think, *Wait, they want my job?*" and immediately shift into self-preservation mode. Big mistake.

Val, an operations guru and the author of *Clash of the Generations: Managing the New Workplace Reality*, knew better. *"Your job,"* she told me, *"isn't to hoard talent. It's to build it."* She spoke from experience. She'd managed teams packed with ambitious and driven millennials at Oxygen Media**,** a company where 56% of the workforce belonged to that generation.

And her philosophy? Lean in. Feed that ambition. Encourage it.

"Absolutely, I'll help you be CEO," she told them. *"It's probably not going to be here, because, let's face it, 50 people are in line before you. But I can teach you how to be a CEO when you start your own company. And then, when you make it big, you can hire me!"*

Val wasn't just offering guidance. She was making a bold, lifelong investment in her people.

Helping Others Grow Helps You Grow

Her approach turned career conversations into an actual develop-ment pipeline, one where employees don't just wait for promotions, they prepare for them. And here's what might surprise you; helping people grow doesn't make them leave faster. It actually does the opposite. It cements loyalty.

The best leaders understand this. They don't see talent development as a threat. They see it as a strategy.

Managers who stifle their people, who keep them trapped in the same role out of fear of losing them, aren't securing their own position. They're sabotaging it.

Val laid it out. *"They won't promote you if there's no one behind you to take your place."*

Translation – if you hoard knowledge, if you block people from growing, you're not getting promoted. You're getting stuck.

That truth stung a little. But it also made total sense.

The CEO Mindset: (Even If You Never Become One)

The magic in Val's approach wasn't just helping young professionals aim high. It was helping them think like a CEO, regardless of their career path.

Not everyone wants to be in the C-Suite. Some people love being high-impact individual contributors and would rather refine their craft than chase a corner office.

And that's fine. But whether someone is climbing the ladder or deepening their expertise, they still need ownership over their career.

"Focus on career development," Val insisted. *"Have consistent conversations with your people. Find out what they want to learn."*

And once you know what drives them, find ways to stretch them; projects, challenges, leadership opportunities, anything that forces them to think bigger, make strategic decisions, and navigate uncertainty.

Because that's what separates stagnant employees from high performers.

MANAGE SELF, LEAD OTHERS

A Manager's Duty: Keep that CV Alive

Then she hit me with another truth bomb.

"As a leader," she said, *"you have a duty to keep your employees' CVs marketable."*

Let that sink in.

Most managers think only about extracting maximum effort from their teams. But the best leaders, the ones people actually want to work for, see their role differently. They don't just think, How can I get the most out of this person? They think:

- How can I make sure this person leaves my team better than when they arrived?

- What experiences can I give them that will make them more valuable in the long run?

- How can I position them to succeed, even if it's not with me?

That's next-level leadership.

It's the difference between transactional management (*Do your job or else.*) and transformational leadership (*I'll help you grow, and you'll want to stay.*).

The Simon Sinek Perspective: "Sailing in the Storm"

Val's insights reminded me of how Simon Sinek describes early-career professionals who expect rapid promotion without enough real-world battle scars.

They say things like, *"I do the same job as Nina, why don't I get paid the same?"* Brian explained.

"But here's the thing. Nina has sailed in the storm. She's made tough calls, managed crises, navigated uncertainty. She's been through the messy, painful, real parts of leadership that younger professionals haven't faced yet."

That's why experience matters.

And that's why Val's approach works so well. She doesn't just teach skills, she creates experiences forcing people to think, react and adapt.

Because that's what real leadership is. Not just knowing the answers but knowing how to navigate the unknown.

Final Takeaway: Leadership Is a Legacy

If you hoard knowledge, if you stunt your team's growth, you don't look stronger, you look insecure.

Great leaders multiply success. They invest in their people because they understand that their legacy is defined not by what they do, but by who they help.

Val Grubb wasn't just talking about training people.

She was talking about creating leaders.

And that's a whole different game.

FEEDBACK

This chapter has perspectives on feedback that intersect like tributaries of the same river.

Tricia Benn agrees performance reviews have become as welcome as going to the dentist; anxiety inducing and demoralizing. It's time to bring in collaborative feedback methods.

Corey Jones anchors feedback firmly in leadership reality; direct, frequent conversations building trust and clarity, and reframing feedback from criticism into strategic growth.

Mel Kettle tackles the often-overlooked side; how to genuinely receive feedback, pushing past defensiveness into open-minded curiosity.

Stacey Hanke emphasizes feedback as personal branding; asking boldly, clearly, and proactively, while always aligning with your desired reputation.

Each expert agrees on one truth: feedback, done right, isn't a judgment; it's a conversation. And conversations are the heartbeat of real leadership.

Episode 22:
Co-Elevating Your Team

Tricia Benn

Performance reviews don't have to feel like a dreaded dentist visit – painful, anxiety-inducing, and leaving you wishing you'd called in sick. According to Tricia Benn, CEO of the C-Suite Network, the secret sauce is to turn performance conversations into authentic dialogues that actually energize people, not drain them.

Dump the medieval torture of hoarding negative feedback all year long just to unleash it in one brutal session. Tricia argues that's not feedback, it's sabotage. Instead, she suggests a more fluid, tailored approach. There's no magic formula or silver bullet here; leadership isn't one-size-fits-all.

It's deeply personal, and your feedback style should reflect who you are as a leader, embracing the messy authenticity that makes great leadership possible.

Tricia advocates a radically collaborative method. Let team members draft their own performance narratives. This shifts the entire dynamic, transforming what once felt like a judgment day into a meaningful conversation built around mutual respect and shared goals.

Quick, frequent check-ins are your friend; short, sharp, and to the point. Weekly or bi-weekly touchpoints help you catch issues early, maintaining clarity and alignment without the drama. No need for lengthy bureaucratic processes when regular conversations do the trick.

In today's era of remote and hybrid work, being intentional about these interactions is key. Tricia insists investing time in regular meetings, even if it feels resource-heavy, is critical to maintaining culture and connection. Yes, it might seem like a lot, but skipping these conversations means risking misalignment, confusion, and disengagement.

Ultimately, Tricia believes true leaders don't just collect followers, they cultivate other leaders. It's less about criticism and more about collaboration. So ditch the rigid playbook and embrace conversations that fuel growth, respect individual.

Episode 122:
HEARTI: 6 Leadership Traits

Corey Jones

The Real Art of Seeking Feedback

Some leaders avoid feedback like it's a bad review waiting to happen. Corey Jones isn't one of them. In Intentional Power, he frames feedback not as critique but as clarity. It's a lifeline for leaders willing to evolve. And let's be honest, evolving isn't optional anymore. It's the cost of admission for modern leadership.

As Corey put it, *"Feedback is like a lifeline to your own growth."* A driver may have side mirrors and a rearview mirror, but there are still blind spots. To see clearly, sometimes you have to turn your head. Or better yet, ask someone riding beside you.

Because here's the truth: Feedback isn't a threat. It's your rearview mirror and your blind spot check.

That means asking directly:

"How am I doing?"

"What needs to change?"

"How am I helping you succeed?"

Notice the tone here. This isn't grovelling, it's grounded. It's leadership with backbone and humility. Feedback doesn't have to be all red ink and rebuke. Sometimes, it's about reinforcing what's working.

In our conversation, I asked Corey the real question that's often left unspoken:

"Asking for feedback implies that you trust you've got an adult-to-adult relationship. How important are brief one-on-one meetings with your direct reports, and what's the right frequency?"

His answer didn't flinch. *"It's imperative,"* he said. Monthly at a minimum, more if you can swing it. You're not just looking for updates ... you're feeling the pulse. What's working? What's not? What's simmering under the surface?

And here's where Corey gets brutally real. In some organizations, open feedback in a group setting can work. But in many? It's a firing squad. Toxic politics, hidden agendas, and performative games make it unsafe. That's why one-on-ones matter. They're not just check-ins. They're trust deposits in the emotional bank account.

Which is why I often say, if you're afraid to ask how you're doing, you're probably overdue.

Corey's takeaway: ask with intent, listen without defensiveness, and be prepared to explain, adjust, or own your part. Feedback isn't weakness. It's strategy.

Episode 130:
Feedback: Giving and Receiving

Mel Kettle

Receiving Feedback Without Falling Apart

If Corey Jones got us thinking about the why of feedback, Mel Kettle hits us with the how, (and not in the usual bullet-point-on-a-slide-deck kind of way). She walked the fire … burnout, stress, loneliness. That's not theory; that's origin story. And it's exactly why she champions self-leadership as the first step to leading others.

When we spoke, Mel didn't start with giving feedback. She started with receiving it. Because that's the blind spot. The overlooked muscle most leaders never train.

"There's so much talk about how to give feedback," she said. *"But how do you receive it? That's the skill people ignore. And it's the harder one."*

And she's right. A lot of us hear the word feedback and our stomach drops. Fight or flight kicks in. We assume something's wrong; something we've done wrong.

"I'd love a better word," she said. *"Feedback can trigger panic. But if you build a culture of real conversation, you might not need the word at all."*

She isn't suggesting we tiptoe around the truth. In fact, quite the opposite. Mel's 5-step framework for receiving feedback doesn't sugar-coat a thing. It just helps you keep your dignity intact while you're learning what you don't want to hear.

Here's how it breaks down:

Step One: **Connect**

Before anything else, understand yourself. Your triggers, your internal stories about feedback, what makes you shut down, what sends you into defence mode. If you know your own wiring, you can stay grounded when someone lights a match.

Step Two: **Set the Scene**

Language matters, setting matters, and timing is everything. Don't start with *"I need to give you feedback"* like you're handing out a pink slip. Try neutral phrasing. *"Can we talk through the project update?"* This keeps people open instead of armored.

Step Three: **Focus on Facts**

Feedback isn't opinion. It's not gossip. And it's not a grudge you've been bottling for 6 months. If you can't anchor it to behavior and impact, it's not feedback. It's venting.

Step 4: **Ask, Listen, Observe**

Mel's big on watching what's not being said. What's happening with body language – silence, tension. If you're receiving feedback, ask follow-up questions so you don't just nod and walk away with the wrong idea. If you're giving it, make sure the message lands. Don't assume it did.

Step 5: **Set Future Goals**

This is the part too many skip. Once the feedback's been given, what now? What's the action plan? What support is needed? Who's doing what? Feedback without follow-through is just noise.

Mel also made it clear that how you give or receive feedback depends entirely on the level of trust. If there's deep trust, an email might be fine. If there's none? Best book a face-to-face and tread carefully. Because, as she put it, *"Clear is kind. Unclear is unkind."* (A nod to Brené Brown landed.)

And what if feedback isn't safe? What if you've got a manager who constantly undermines you in meetings, then plays innocent later?

Mel's advice is to start with curiosity, not confrontation. Assume they're unaware before you assume they're malicious. But if it keeps happening – if they know, and they keep doing it – then you've got a different problem; and maybe a bigger decision to make.

"Sometimes feedback isn't the issue," she said. *"It's the system around it, the culture, the silence, the fear."*

And in those cases? You might be better off finding another table to sit at.

Mel reminds us that feedback isn't just a tool. It's a test of trust, of timing, of how much emotional intelligence a workplace really has, not just claims to have. The 5-step framework gives us a way forward. But more than that, it asks us to be human first, leader second.

As we continue exploring the role of feedback in leadership, it's clear that how we give and receive it tells the truth about our culture, our courage, and our connection to the people we lead.

Episode 156:
Influence Elevated

Stacy Hanke

Stacey Hanke isn't your average corporate guru. She's a Hall of Fame speaker who turns the standard script upside down. While everyone's busy climbing ladders, chasing titles, or building a career brand, Stacey reminds us; your personal brand isn't something the company owns. It's yours. You cultivate it, protect it, and leverage it, whether you're eyeing the top spot or planning your next side move.

And if you really want executive presence, you'd better actually be present. No sneaky email-checking, no multitasking under the table, and please, turn your camera on in virtual meetings. Show up fully, respect the room, or don't show up at all.

Feedback? Stacey has 0 patience for vague niceties or passive-aggressive games. Be direct, be specific, and if you're receiving feedback, actively ask for it. Say precisely what you need, whether it's your tone, your body language, or clarity of your message. Stacey suggests saying something like, *"Here's what I'm working on. Would you watch for that?"* or more directly, *"What specific feedback have you received in the past on how you deliver a message?"* She's all about creating clarity up-front, setting expectations so the feedback is genuinely useful.

Her golden rule? Feedback isn't a one-way street; it moves up, down, and sideways. Leaders who never ask for feedback themselves breed cultures of polite dishonesty. Stacey lives by this, constantly asking her own team, *"What specifically do you want to improve on when it comes to your messaging?"* It's always mutual; never top-down.

Most importantly, feedback should align with your personal brand – who you are, where you're heading, and how you want others to see you. Stacey doesn't just preach influence, she lives it. Clear, targeted feedback isn't criticism; it's fuel for growth.

So, figure out your brand first. Then, and only then, can you hold yourself and others truly accountable.

Episode 79:
Belonging and Culture

Fiona Robertson

The Price of Belonging

Culture isn't beanbags, beers, or mission statements in calligraphy. Culture is pain and safety and rules of engagement coded deep into our nervous systems. Fiona Robertson sees culture not as an initiative or a vibe, but as a series of unconscious agreements about what earns you belonging and what gets you quietly pushed out. As former Head of Culture at one of Australia's Big Four banks, National Australia Bank, she's seen it up close – powerful, messy and often invisible to the people it governs.

In her book *Rules of Belonging*, Fiona doesn't just map the terrain, she hands you the flashlight, the compass and the questions that crack open the walls. It's not theory, it's how-to.

Culture Hides in Plain Sight

You can't fix what you can't see. Most leaders talk about culture, but few can define it. *"That's the trap,"* Fiona says. *"Culture is the interpretation of behaviour, not the behaviour itself."* A senior leader walking out of a meeting before it ends might be seen as high status in one culture, or deeply disrespectful in another. Same action, different cultural coding.

Which is why culture change starts with decoding those micro-signals of what earns you status and inclusion. What gets you safe? What gets you sidelined?

The Biology of Belonging

Maslow had it wrong. Belonging doesn't come *after* food, water, and shelter; it comes *before*. Neuroscience now tells us the human brain doesn't differentiate between physical pain and social pain. Being excluded from a meeting or ignored in a brainstorm triggers the same neurological distress as a broken bone.

That's why candour is so hard. Feedback feels like threat. And leaders who blurt out, *"I just want more honesty around here,"* without creating psychological safety are essentially yelling "jump" at people with no parachute.

Why Candour Feels Like Violence

Fiona doesn't sugar-coat it. Telling the truth at work ... real truth, the kind that challenges, corrects or exposes ... does hurt. Even the *announcement* of feedback causes a spike in stress hormones. Tell someone, *"I've got some feedback for you,"* and their brain processes it like a threat of physical harm. You may as well say, *"I'm about to stab you with a fork."*

This is why teams default to artificial harmony; everyone smiling, nodding and going nowhere.

Collaboration Isn't Kumbaya

Not everyone in a team needs to collaborate on everything. And that's the first mistake many leaders make. Collaboration must be intentional. Ask which initiatives require shared ownership? Once that's clear, Fiona says, assign shared objectives and name a peer leader to drive the process. Then ask the most important question, *"Who needs help this week?"*

It's deceptively simple, and wildly powerful. Because when asking for help becomes the norm not the exception, ego takes a backseat to results, and helping others becomes a badge of honour, not a burden.

Accountability: The Civil Kind

Peer-to-peer accountability is trending, and for good reason. It's agile, fast, and closer to the action. But left unchecked, it can devolve into nitpicking or point-scoring. Fiona warns against peers who *"delight in finding mistakes."* You know the type. She says the line is clear: *play the ball, not the person.* If feedback comes from a place of sabotage, it's poison. But if it's in service of a better outcome, it's culture gold.

The litmus test? Motivation. If your aim is to help your peer succeed, call it out. If your aim is to make yourself look good by comparison, sit down.

Leaders Set the Standard by What They Tolerate

When leaders ignore subtle digs, passive blame, or perfectionist panic, they signal that this is how we do things around here. That's dangerous. Teams watch everything, especially what their leaders silently condone.

Fiona uses the analogy of kids pointing fingers at each other. *"He started it!" "It wasn't my fault!"* If a leader tolerates that, the team becomes a pack of toddlers. But if the leader says, *"Not interested in blame; we solve this together,"* the tone shifts. Fast.

Mistakes Aren't Sins

Mistake tolerance isn't optional. It's oxygen, because if people are afraid to make a mistake, they're afraid to try. And that fear will choke innovation before it's even lit. Fiona's rule: if someone owns a mistake, the leader's job is not to punish, it's to debrief, reflect and make sure it becomes part of collective learning.

And if the leader mishandles a mistake in the heat of the moment? Apologise. Say it out loud, *"I got that wrong. That wasn't how I want us to handle mistakes in this team."* It's not weakness. It's leadership with a spine.

Reward What You Want Repeated

Social rewards are stronger than cash. If helping each other is the goal, then celebrate the helpers. It doesn't have to be a trophy, it can be praise. *"What you did helped the whole team move forward."* Say it out loud. Say it often. People will model what gets noticed.

SELF-LEADERSHIP

Episode 137:
Crucial Conversations

Andrew Bryant

Andrew Bryant defines self-leadership as *"the practice of intentionally influencing your thinking, feeling and actions toward your objectives."* And it begins with self-awareness: knowing what you think and feel, and being honest about how those internal states shape your external results.

Throughout our conversation, Bryant repeatedly circled back to this key idea of intentionality. Self-leadership is not reactive. It's proactive. It asks the question: *"Who am I becoming?"* and *"What impact am I having?"* Every word, every action, is a choice. And with choice comes responsibility. *"You're not responsible for others,"* he explains, *"but you are accountable to your agreements with them."* That distinction matters.

Linking ancient wisdom to modern complexity, Bryant points to Stoic philosophy, particularly the teachings of Epictetus: *"It's not what happens to you, but how you respond."* Self-leadership, like Stoicism, isn't about controlling the world. It's about controlling your inner world, owning your mindset, regulating your emotions and learning from every situation.

He also underscores the importance of decision-making. True self-leaders don't wait for perfect certainty before acting. Elite leaders often move forward with just 60 – 65% certainty, knowing they can course-correct along the way. Waiting for 99.9% certainty, Andrew warns, is the territory of bureaucrats paralyzed by fear.

We also explored the overlap between emotional intelligence and self-leadership. Emotional intelligence is about recognising and regulating your emotions. Self-leadership goes further, using emotional insight to steer your choices intentionally. One is reactive. The other is intentional.

Ultimately, Andrew's message is simple, but not easy: *You are the driver of your life. If you don't lead yourself, someone else will.* Self-leadership is a daily practice. It doesn't happen by accident. And it's the foundation for leading others with integrity, wisdom, and clarity.

Episode 113:
Showing Up As Yourself

Lynell Green

Finding Your Voice Before You Lose It

Lynell Green, with 4 decades of lived experience in corporate life, now helps leaders, emerging and executive, strip off the imitation game and confront the uncomfortable truth: you can't lead effectively trying to fit into someone else's shoes.

Here's the core of her message: leadership isn't just putting on a uniform. Trying to emulate your favorite CEO (whether it's Zuckerberg, Sheryl Sandberg or your old boss from 5 years ago) is the fast-track to irrelevance. Their moves aren't your moves. Their tone doesn't match your voice. And your team? They can intuit inauthenticity a mile off.

So what's the fix? Start with what's real. Lynell begins by locating "the gap," the space between where a leader is and where they want to be. And she doesn't fill it with fluff or 10-step plans. She helps them build strategies based on experiences they need and relationships they must cultivate, from peers to senior executives; because everyone, from cleaner to CEO, is part of the workplace ecosystem. You don't get to opt out.

But here's where it gets juicy. Lynell is a pattern spotter. She sees what leaders often miss: their recurring blind spots, behaviors that sabotage them over and over. Leaders who defer, shrink or dim their light to smooth things over aren't "team players." They're hiding; and hiding gets you nowhere.

Lynell's take? *"You have to shine brighter to be seen. Hiding behind someone else's brightness doesn't work."* That's not a metaphor; that's a call to action.

And what about those "hard conversations" that everyone dreads? That's where the game changes. If you walk into it saying, *"This will be hard,"* you've already sabotaged yourself. Context is decisive. Change your mindset, and you change the outcome.

Let's say your manager is micromanaging you. Most people stew or complain to peers. Lynell coaches you to flip the lens to ask, why might they be micromanaging? Maybe you dropped the ball before. Maybe they don't trust you … yet. Instead of storming in with blame, try, *"I've created a progress document. I notice you still check-in frequently. Is there something I can improve to earn your confidence back?"* That's clarity, that's ownership, and that's leadership.

She's also big on rehearsing exactly what to say; not to become robotic, but to sound natural *on purpose.* Our brains tend to exaggerate what could go wrong. So, when you don't practice, your subconscious turns that meeting into a scary movie. But when you've got a few go-to lines in your toolkit? You stop flinching and start leading.

For example, if meetings drag because someone's over-talking, Lynell arms you with a line like: *"That's a great point, Bob. Can I interject here?"* It's graceful, it's effective, and it stops the monologue without collateral damage.

Lynell's philosophy is grounded in a powerful reframe of using tools, instead of weapons. Your communication isn't for cutting people down. It's for lifting performance and protecting your leadership integrity.

And no, she doesn't offer one-size-fits-all frameworks. Her work is tailored to each person, intuitive and deeply personal. Each client creates their own strategy for growth, based on what they want, who they are and where they're heading. It's not about chasing titles. It's about mastering self-expression and owning your voice in any room you walk into.

To sum it up, Lynell Green doesn't teach leadership. She extracts it – from the blind spots, the breakdowns, the dodged conversations and the borrowed personas. Because if you're not leading from your own center, you're not really leading at all.

Episode 144:
The Multi-Dimensional Leader

Dan Silberberg

Beyond Hierarchy, Beyond Ego

Let's get one thing straight: traditional leadership is dead; or at least, it should be.

The old playbook – command and control, top-down hierarchy, carrot-and-stick incentives – is still limping along in some outdated corporate corners. But in a VUCA world defined by volatility, uncertainty, complexity and ambiguity, a leader stuck in the 3-dimensional model is leading their company off a cliff.

Dan Silberberg, CEO whisperer and intellectual force of nature, doesn't mince words. His message? Stop playing small. Stop managing through coercion. Stop pretending the world hasn't changed.

Because it has.

And if you're still clinging to legacy leadership models, you're already obsolete.

Hierarchies Are for Dinosaurs

For decades, corporate leadership operated on a simple but flawed premise:

1. Pick a leadership style – transformational, servant, directive, charismatic.

2. Develop some traits – confidence, decisiveness, strategic thinking.

3. Acquire skills – public speaking, negotiation, financial acumen.

That's the 3-dimensional model, the one leadership schools peddle. And for a while, it worked.

Companies functioned like industrial-era machines, assembly lines of human effort. Managers supervised. Employees obeyed. Efficiency was everything.

But then came disruption.

The world flipped.

Customers demanded more ... more transparency, more ethics, more innovation. Employees started walking away from toxic workplaces, refusing to dedicate their lives to corporate machines that saw them as expendable.

And yet, some leaders still sit in their glass offices, pretending they have control.

They don't.

What they do have, if they're not careful, is a ship full of disengaged employees, quietly plotting their escape while pretending to care in Zoom meetings.

"73% of people," Dan said, *"are unengaged in their work."*

Not just bored. Unengaged and mentally checked out; clocking in and out like ghosts.

Even worse? 20% actively sabotage the business.

Why? Because they resent it.

Poor leadership doesn't just create mediocre workplaces; it creates open rebellion.

And if you think your traditional, hierarchy-driven *"I'm the boss, do what I say"* model is keeping people in line, you're delusional.

They're not in line. They're plotting their exit.

From Coercion to Ecosystem: A New Power Structure

Dan's proposition is simple but radical: kill the hierarchy, build an ecosystem.

Instead of a top-down command structure, he proposes something more organic, more fluid, more adaptive.

An ecosystem, where:

- Power isn't hoarded; it's distributed.
- People don't need permission to think, they own their work.
- Decisions aren't dictated from above. They emerge from collective intelligence.

In a rigid hierarchy, employees hide problems from their managers out of fear.

In an ecosystem, employees solve problems because they feel trusted and empowered.

And trust? That's the currency of 21st-century leadership.

"In a hierarchy," Dan says, *"leaders don't trust their teams. That's why they build silos, guardrails, and layers of bureaucracy."*

It's control-freak leadership, and it kills innovation.

Want proof? Look at middle management, the corporate layer designed mostly to chase deadlines, micromanage, and ensure compliance.

"What do middle managers actually do?" Dan asks. *"Mostly, they're the accountability police. They ask, Hey, Nina, how's that project going? Will it be done by Wednesday?"*

That's not leadership. That's administration.

In an ecosystem, accountability is peer-driven, not enforced from above. People don't need a boss breathing down their necks to stay on track. They own their responsibilities because they have actual autonomy.

That's how real engagement happens, not through perks, not through forced fun, but through ownership.

And yet, the old guard still clings to coercion as their power strategy.

Which brings us to the real question every leader should ask themselves:

What's Your Relationship to Power?

Dan isn't afraid to ask the big, uncomfortable questions.

And this one cuts deep: as a leader, what's your relationship to power?

Are you:

- A control freak who hoards decisions and resists change?
- A gladiator-style boss who thrives on internal competition?
- An insecure leader who plays politics and stifles talent?

Or are you:

- A mentor helping others grow, even beyond you?
- A coach removing obstacles instead of creating them?
- A catalyst igniting potential instead of suppressing it?

The command-and-control model was built on a scarcity mindset; the belief that power is a finite resource to be guarded, not shared.

But the best leaders – multi-dimensional leaders – know that power is a multiplier. The more you empower others, the stronger your leadership becomes.

The Inner Work of Leadership

This is where Dan flips leadership development on its head.

Forget executive coaching, 360 degree reviews or performance metrics. The real question isn't what kind of leader are you? It's who are you, period?

Leadership isn't about traits or skills. It's about being ...

- Are you self-aware?
- Do you know your triggers?
- Do you understand your blind spots?

If not, your leadership is reactive, not intentional.
And reactive leaders? They're dangerous.
They:

- Take criticism personally
- Pass their stress onto their teams
- Make emotionally-driven decisions
- Default to blame instead of self-reflection

"Most people," Dan said, *"spend their lives in reactivity, not intentionality."*
Multi-dimensional leaders? They flip that equation.

- They cultivate self-mastery.
- They don't get hijacked by their emotions.
- They don't let ego drive decisions.
- And they absolutely don't weaponize power.

The Leadership Shift Is Already Happening

Traditional leadership is unravelling. People aren't tolerating toxic workplaces, outdated power structures, or rigid corporate silos anymore. They're walking away.

And leaders who refuse to evolve will get left behind.

The multi-dimensional leader – the one who leads through trust, autonomy, and self-awareness – isn't a nice-to-have.

It's the only way forward.

The question isn't, *"Will you embrace this?"*

The question is, *"How long can you survive if you don't?"*

Episode 112:
Childhood Triggers
Controlling Us

Onno Koelman

The Invisible Backpack We Carry

Ever notice how some people snap under pressure while others stay cool as a cucumber? Or how some leaders lean into conflict while others avoid it like a ticking time bomb?

Turns out, a lot of it has nothing to do with skillset or strategy, but everything to do with what's lurking in our invisible backpack.

That's the term Onno Koelman uses to describe the beliefs, assumptions and emotional triggers we accumulate over a lifetime. Some we pick up as kids, some as young professionals, and some we don't even realize we're carrying.

But make no mistake, those hidden beliefs run the show.

If you grew up in a household where conflict meant raised voices and slammed doors, you might carry an invisible rule, conflict is dangerous, avoid at all costs.

Fast-forward to the workplace and suddenly you're the manager who can't hold people accountable.

Or maybe you learned as a kid that the world is unsafe and people are out to get you. Now every harmless critique feels like an attack, every missed email like a sign of disrespect. You see hidden agendas everywhere.

But understand this. Most of us have no idea these beliefs exist.

They just operate in the background, shaping our emotions, behaviors and decisions, often in ways that sabotage our leadership.

Triggers: The Stories We Tell Ourselves

Let's talk about the snake in the grass.

Onno paints a vivid picture: You're out for a walk. You see something long, brown, and coiled up on the trail. Your brain screams "SNAKE!" and adrenaline floods your system. Your body tenses, your heart pounds, you freeze.

But then ... the "snake" doesn't move.

You squint.

It's a stick.

In an instant, the fear dissolves, your body relaxes. The emotional reaction, so intense just moments ago, vanishes into thin air.

Here's what happened in 4 simple steps:

> Data – you saw something brown and squiggly.
> Thought – "that's a snake!"
> Emotion – fear, panic, fight-or-flight mode.
> Reaction – freeze, back away, heart pounding.

But the only thing that actually changed was your thought. The data was the same, a brown squiggly thing in the dirt. The difference was how your brain interpreted it.

"And that," Onno says, *"is the key to understanding our triggers."*

We don't react to what happens. We react to the meaning we assign to what happens.

From Fear to False Narratives

Now, let's apply that to leadership.

Imagine a manager who says:

"My team doesn't respect me. They ignore my emails."

> What's the data?
> Emails aren't getting answered.

> What's the thought?
> They must not respect me.

What's the emotion?
Frustration, resentment, insecurity.

What's the reaction?
Micromanage. Withdraw. Assume the worst.

But what if the thought was wrong?

Maybe people aren't ignoring the manager on purpose. They're just overwhelmed, prioritizing client emails first or missing messages in a cluttered inbox.

The truth is, leaders make up stories all the time. And unless we check those stories against reality, we can end up damaging relationships, misinterpreting behaviors and making terrible leadership decisions.

Paradigms: The Rules We Didn't Know We Wrote

Triggers don't exist in a vacuum. They're part of a bigger system of beliefs, what Onno has been trained to identify as *paradigms*.

The concept of identifying and coaching for paradigm shifts was beautifully laid out by Dr. Keith Merron in his book, *The Art of Transformational Coaching.*

Paradigms are the deep-rooted mental models we use to navigate the world.

- If your paradigm is "All conflict is bad," you will do everything in your power to avoid it, even when direct feedback is exactly what your team needs.

- If your paradigm is "People are out to get me," you will interpret neutral actions as hostile, creating unnecessary tension.

- If your paradigm is "I must prove my worth every day," you will overwork, overcompensate, and never feel good enough, no matter how much you accomplish.

The solution?

Upgrade the paradigm.

Just like software, our mental models need updates.

Leaders who outgrow their old paradigms and install new ones become more effective, resilient, and emotionally intelligent.

The work starts with one key question:

"Is this belief still serving me?"

The Psychological Immune System

Here's why leadership transformation is hard: Your brain fights it.

Onno refers to the psychological immune system, a term popularized by Kegan and Lahey in their book *"The Immunity to Change."* It's an invisible force designed to keep you safe.

- It stops you from taking risks that might backfire.

- It protects you from the pain of failure or rejection.

- It warns you against stepping outside your comfort zone.

Which is great ... except when it's keeping you small.

Onno gives an example. As a child a young professional watched their parents argue constantly.

Their psychological immune system forms a rule: conflict is dangerous. Avoid it at all costs.

This rule worked as a kid; staying quiet kept them safe.

But now they're a manager and suddenly avoiding conflict means:

- They don't hold their team accountable.

- They sugarcoat feedback until it's useless.

- They settle for "artificial harmony" instead of real conversations.

What once kept them safe is now holding them back. That's the immunity to change. It's why New Year's resolutions fail and why poor leadership habits stick around for years.

And it's why true leadership growth requires more than just skill-building. It demands deep, internal work to rewrite those outdated rules.

Leaders Bring the Weather with Them

If there's one line Onno keeps coming back to, it's this ... Leaders bring the weather with them. Like it or not, emotions are contagious.

If a leader is calm under pressure, the team stays steady. If a leader is panicked and reactive, chaos spreads like wildfire. If a leader is cynical and distrusting, people shut down, disengage and stop contributing.

Leadership isn't just about strategy. It's about emotional climate control.

Great leaders:

- recognize their triggers before they hijack a situation.

- challenge their assumptions before reacting.

- rewire old paradigms that no longer serve them.

- bring self-awareness to the table so their emotions don't poison the culture.

Because at the end of the day, leadership isn't about controlling people.

It's about controlling yourself so you can lead with clarity, wisdom and purpose.

And that starts inside the invisible backpack.

Final Thought: Your Triggers Are Not Your Truth

Onno Koelman's insights make one thing clear – your triggers are not your truth.

They are simply automatic responses based on past experiences.

But here's the thing.

- Just because you feel disrespected doesn't mean you are.

- Just because conflict makes you uncomfortable doesn't mean it's bad.

- Just because leadership is hard doesn't mean you're failing.

The best leaders don't just react to their emotions.

They investigate them.

And in that space – between trigger and reaction – is where real leadership happens.

Episode 36:
Beyond the Military Model
of Leadership

Bob Pizzini

The Physiology of Self-Leadership

If you want to know what keeps a former Navy SEAL grounded in the boardroom, it's not bravado or buzzwords. It's 6 deceptively simple disciplines: rest, hydration, nutrition, exercise, brain and heart health, and lifelong learning. Bob Pizzini doesn't deliver leadership theory from a pedestal. He brings it in a flight suit, tempered by skydives, close calls, and leading teams where hesitation could be fatal.

The Van Analogy

He calls it the science of leadership, but don't mistake that for sterile. These 6 factors, he says, are so interwoven that he visualizes them as the tires on a van. One goes flat, they all go wobbly. If you're underslept and dehydrated, no number of motivational posters will fix your poor decisions. It's leadership through physiology, and it's foundational.

"You want to be a high-performance leader? Then treat yourself like a high-performance machine," Bob says, straight up. The irony isn't lost. Most leaders pay more attention to their inbox than their intake. But not Bob. He's built *Elevate Your Leadership*, his training program, around these 6 pillars. As he puts it, *"leadership is not complex, but it sure isn't easy."*

Building His Own Model

He didn't find what he needed in traditional leadership training, so he built it himself. Military-style, practical, and repeatable. He wanted tools that leaders could deploy like a weapon in the fog of decision-making. And to keep it grounded, he tossed in indoor skydiving. Yes, really. His workshops aren't death-by-slide-deck. They're kinetic. Participants literally take flight. Because stretching your comfort zone, Bob argues, is the only way to expand it.

Making Mistakes, Owning Mistakes

But he's not all grit and adrenaline. He's clear that leadership is imperfect because people are imperfect. Mistakes happen. Leaders make them. Teams make them. The defining factor isn't the error. It's how you respond. If your people make a mistake, assume it wasn't malicious; 95% of the time, he says, it isn't. So own your screw-ups, apologize fast, and move on.

The Power of Metacognition

That ability to pause and self-correct is what Bob calls **metacognition**, thinking about your thinking. It's not some naval-gazing indulgence. It's what separates weak leaders from the strong. Reflection, self-awareness, courage to admit when they got it wrong. *"The weaker leaders,"* he says, *"don't reflect. They just react."* In his world, that's a liability.

Mono. Stereo. Surround Sound.

Bob believes leadership starts with self-leadership. Mono. Then stereo. Then surround sound. In mono, you ask: Am I rested? Hydrated? Nourished? In stereo: Is the person across from me okay, physically, mentally? And surround sound? That's when you scale it across your team or organization. You build a culture where wellness isn't lip service. It's part of the infrastructure.

Books that Build Resilience

And when you ask Bob what he reads? It's not the usual business bestsellers. His go-tos are van der Kolk's *The Body Keeps the Score* and *Unstuck* – books about trauma, resilience, and how the human system recovers from breakdown. He's not reading for quick wins. He's reading to understand what makes people break and how they heal. That's what a real leader does.

The Daily Practice of Leadership

Leadership, to Bob, is not just a role. It's a choice, made daily, supported by a system of habits. You don't have to skydive to get it. But you do have to get out of your comfort zone, build your own blueprint, and monitor your mental and physical state. Reflect. Apologize. Learn. Repeat. Every day.

"Lifelong learning is a key component of lifelong leadership," Bob says, as casually as if he were handing you a glass of water. And that's what sticks. This isn't pep talk leadership. This is ground-up, guts-and-grit leadership. Not polished, not perfect, but fiercely human.

And in today's world, that might just be the highest form of leadership we've got.

Episode 92:
Mind-Bending Neuro-Insights

Allan Parker OAM

When it comes to self-leadership, few bring the gravitas, wit and brain science credibility of Allan Parker OAM. Awarded the Order of Australia Medal for his contributions to business and dispute resolution, Allan is a behavioural scientist, marathon runner, scratch golfer and master communicator who doesn't just talk about leadership, he embodies it.

In our conversation, Allan brought his signature mix of neuroscience and deep humility to the forefront, sharing practical techniques that challenge traditional leadership norms. From speculative language and permission-based communication to pausing for impact, Allan's methodology reveals how subtle shifts in how we speak, listen, and question can dramatically improve how we lead ourselves and others.

Knowing Yourself Before Leading Others

Allan's philosophy begins with a simple but profound truth: *"I can only bring about the change in others that I can demonstrate in myself."* Self-leadership, he argues, is not about having a rigid personality type or adhering to a fixed leadership style. In fact, he critiques the overemphasis on personality assessments in the corporate world. *"We got too caught up in personality. Personality is what I arrived with. But who I am is not fixed."*

Instead, Allan advocates for neuroplasticity, the brain's ability to change, learn, and grow. He reminds us that we all have billions of neurons waiting to be engaged, but the trouble is, we often don't know how to access them.

Hydration, Oxygen, and Brain Function

With his leadership advice grounded in biology, Allan's go-to message is, drink more water. That might seem unorthodox, but his explanation is rooted in neuroscience. Hydration delivers oxygen to the brain which fuels the glucose conversion process producing glutamate, a neurotransmitter responsible for clear thinking. Without enough water, the brain underperforms. And it only takes a cup of coffee or a glass of wine to begin the dehydration process. *"I don't tell people to stop anything,"* Allan says. *"I just tell them to add more."*

The Power of Speculative Language

One of Allan's most powerful techniques is the use of speculative language: would, could, and might. These words activate the brain's curiosity and allow ideas to be explored without the fear of being wrong. They remove the binary of right or wrong and foster innovation.

For example, instead of saying, *"What will we do?"* Allan reframes it as, *"What might we be able to do here?"* This subtle shift opens the door for diverse perspectives, especially in multicultural or indirect communication cultures where saving face is vital.

Creating Conversational Equality

Allan has a bone to pick with meetings where extroverts dominate. He speaks passionately about the missed opportunities when introverts stay silent.

Innovation walks out of every meeting in the heads of the introverts.
—Allan Parker

His approach to conversational equality is both philosophical and practical.

He recommends managers proactively create space for every voice to be heard. This might mean pausing more, inviting quieter team members to share their thoughts, or asking directly, *"What do you think, Jane? What do you think, Jack?"*

He also teaches introverts a strategy for respectfully interrupting fast talkers: wait for the speaker to inhale, then interject with a name and a question. For example, *"Nina, I'm just wondering ... would it be okay if I asked a question about that?"* That tiny window of breath is a powerful gateway to enter the conversation.

Timing, Permission, and Inquiry

Allan's framework for respectful and impactful communication includes 3 cornerstones: timing, permission, and genuine inquiry.

> Watch for the moment to speak.
> Ask for permission to engage.
> Then lean into curiosity.

He often uses phrases like, *"I'm just wondering ... "* or *"I have a suspicion that ... "* which gently invite collaboration rather than confrontation. These are not manipulative tactics; they are strategic, mindful, and rooted in neuroscience. They help turn meetings into thinking labs where ideas are developed collectively, not dictated from above.

Pacing and Pausing

Too many leaders, Allan warns, speak too quickly. They firehose their audience with words and unintentionally shut down the room. *"The alert system is running the show. We're all reactive. We need to slow it down."*

He teaches the importance of pauses. When someone nods, pause. When someone looks like they're about to speak, pause. This gives space for the listener to process and the conversation to breathe. It also models the self-regulation leaders need if they want to cultivate more meaningful dialogue.

Language that Sparks Innovation

Allan is fascinated by what he calls the "fifth idea." In his work with global organisations, he noticed a pattern. The *first* idea voiced in a meeting is usually safe. The *second* is familiar. The *third* is hesitant. The *fourth* may be hard to articulate. But the *fifth* idea – especially from the quiet thinkers – is often where true innovation lives. Leaders, he says, must go digging for it.

He encourages managers to ask, *"What might be an alternative to that?"* or *"What would be our fallback position?"* These prompts keep the ideation process fluid and reduce the dominance of status-quo thinking.

The Role of the Manager: Facilitator, Not Boss

Allan champions a manager's role as a facilitator of thinking, not an authoritarian. Leaders who foster psychological safety create environments where people feel empowered to speak, question, and reflect. He urges leaders to resist the urge to react immediately and instead model reflection and humility.

"I'm not certain about anything," he laughs. *"Except that I don't know what I thought I knew."*

In a world where meetings are often run on autopilot and innovation is sacrificed at the altar of efficiency, Allan Parker shows us how slowing down, choosing words intentionally, and creating space for all voices can transform leadership from a role into a practice. Self-leadership, he reminds us, begins not just with knowing yourself but with making room for everyone else's brilliance too.

Episode 25:
Self-Leadership

Ian Stephens

The First Team Is You

Ian Stephens doesn't mess around. He'll tell you straight: if you want to lead others, you've got to start with yourself. And not just the shiny bits you post on LinkedIn. We're talking the whole deal. Your discipline. Your state of mind. Your ability to slow down and listen to the quiet hum of your own instincts before the noise of the day drowns them out.

He calls it self-leadership. And when a CEO says to his team, *"It's a given, you must be grounded in self-leadership,"* that's not a polite nudge; that's a mandate.

Evolving or Rotting

If you're not expanding your epistemology – that is, the sum of your knowledge, skills, and experience – then you're stagnating. Ian's words echo what the best managers know but don't always say out loud: evolution is non-negotiable.

Attending technical conferences isn't enough. Mastery of hard skills doesn't make you a good leader. What about the emotional landscape of your team? The interpersonal climate? That's where the real growth lies.

Meet SOL: The Praying Mantis of Self-Leadership

In Ian's book *Shift Culture*, self-leadership has a mascot: a praying mantis named SOL. Not because it's cute, but because it knows how to be still. SOL stands for "Solitude," and it represents a core principle. Successful leaders carve out time – 3 or 4 sessions a week – for silent thinking. No phones, no urgent pings, no one asking for 5 minutes. Just quiet. Long enough for your subconscious to surface with the whispers you're too busy to hear during the day.

Solitude isn't a luxury; it's a survival skill. It's what separates reactive managers from intuitive leaders. That quiet voice might nudge you to follow up with a client, realign a strategy, or call someone who hasn't been on your radar. And it won't show up unless you create the space.

The REAPA Principle: Think Like a Jaguar

Ian introduces another animal into the mix – the jaguar. Sleek, silent, deadly focused. This isn't about aggression. It's about precision. The REAPA principle is a framework for decision-making, and it works like this:

> **R: Relax**. Take a breath. Let tension drop.
> **E: Envision** the outcome you want.
> **A: Assess** your options.
> **P: Patience** to reevaluate before moving.
> **A: Act** only once the rest are complete.

He's seen it time and again; people skip straight to act, then circle back trying to fix what went wrong. They get trapped in a reaction loop. But when you follow REAPA, the outcome is sharper, calmer, and often better.

Getting Out of Your Own Way

Most people think if they're working hard, they're getting closer to a breakthrough. But sometimes, stepping away is the real catalyst. One of Ian's workshop participants was struggling with a project until he took a 30-minute break. The solution hit him as he returned, not while he was grinding.

Thinking by not thinking. That's what REAPA enables.

Managers, Take Note

Want your team to step up in their own self-leadership? Model it. Give permission to pause. Encourage solitude in your workplace. Suggest walking away from the meeting table before deciding something big. Let people *muse*. Build in reflection time instead of packing agendas to the brim. This is how you build thinking managers, not just task machines.

And if you teach your team the REAPA acronym, you'll hear it being used around the office. *"Before we act, let's REAPA this."* Now you've got shared language, and that's cultural gold.

Be Patient. Then Move.

Patience isn't about being passive. It's power in reserve, a conscious pause. Ian reminds us that when you lose patience, your tone, your posture, and your listening skills tank. Self-leadership means noticing that moment and choosing a better response. Take a breath. Take a beat.

Even if it's the end of the year and you're fried, you can own it. Ian does. You just say, *"I think I'm ready for a holiday. I'm sorry I was short with you earlier."* That's not weakness. That's leadership with backbone.

Zen Masters in Boxing Gloves

In one of Ian's keynote routines, he brings out a speedball. And not just as a gimmick. It's a metaphor. At first, people fumble. But within days, they master the rhythm. Why? Because mastery is a process. Apply focus, skill and repetition and the awkward becomes actionable.

Just like leadership, just like life.

CULTURE

Episode 35:
Hero Leadership:
The Hero Factor

Jeffrey Hayzlett

Leadership in the C-Suite:
Beyond the Numbers, Beyond the Ego

There's something about Jeffrey Hayzlett that makes you sit up a little straighter. Maybe it's the energy, the deep-voiced, straight-shooting authority. Maybe it's the cowboy swagger – big, bold and unafraid to tell it like it is.

Whatever it is, Jeffrey isn't just another executive spouting about leadership. He's lived it, sat in the biggest chairs, made the biggest calls, and learned, sometimes the hard way, what separates good leaders from great ones.

And according to him, it's not just operational excellence. It's hero leadership.

Most leaders get stuck chasing performance metrics, operational efficiency and quarterly wins. But Jeffrey's playbook is different. It's built around The Hero Factor, a concept that goes beyond profit margins and stock performance to something far more valuable; leading with values, putting people above profit and building companies that matter.

"The best companies," he says, *"make the most money, have the best culture, and the happiest employees. It's not a coincidence."*

You don't get there by squeezing the last drop out of your workforce. You get there by leading with purpose.

The C-Suite Trap: When Ego Kills Leadership

"What's the one thing leaders are not doing, that they should be doing? I ask. *"Listening."* It sounds simple, but it's deadly.

Too many leaders think they have to be the smartest person in the room. The problem? That chokes innovation, suffocates morale, and creates a toxic "do as I say" culture.

Real leadership, according to Jeffrey, is not about having the answers; it's about asking the right questions.

And yet, ego gets in the way.

Some CEOs cling to power like a drowning man clings to a lifeboat. They're afraid to share the credit, terrified of looking weak.

The irony?

That fear makes them weak. Insecure leaders hoard decisions. Confident leaders empower others.

Jeffrey believes in flipping the script:

- Don't be the boss with all the answers. Be the leader who pulls the best out of their team.

- Don't control people. Inspire them.

- Don't build a cult of personality. Build a culture of trust.

It's not about positioning yourself as the center of the universe.
It's about serving others so they can do their best work.
That's what hero leaders do.

Hero Leaders vs. Operational Leaders

For years, the gold standard in business was operational excellence.
Run lean, cut waste, optimize processes.
Nothing wrong with that.
But Jeffrey argues that if that's all you're pursuing, you're missing the bigger return.

Yes, operational excellence matters, but without values-driven leadership, you're just running a machine. Sooner or later, people burn out, disengage, or jump ship.

Real magic happens when leaders blend operational excellence with hero leadership. That means:

- Values aren't just words on a wall. They're lived every day.
- People aren't just resources. They're the heartbeat of the business.
- Decisions aren't just about the bottom line. They're about long-term impact.

And companies that get this balance right?

They crush their competition.

Because here's the paradox: Businesses that lead with purpose make MORE money, not less.

And Jeffrey has the data to prove it.

Culture Is More Than a Buzzword. It's Your Competitive Edge

Here's a hard truth: Most employees don't know their company's values.

Not because they're lazy. Not because they don't care.

But because no one has ever made them matter.

Too many organizations treat culture like a plaque on the wall, a set of generic words that mean nothing in practice.

Hero leaders don't make that mistake.

They:

- Embed values in everyday decisions.
- Talk about them constantly.
- Hold people accountable when they're ignored.

A company's values define its culture, and its culture defines its success.

Because when people believe in what they're doing, when they feel valued, respected, and part of something bigger, they perform at a higher level.

That's why Jeffrey's companies thrive.

They don't just talk about culture.

They live it.

The Moment that Changed Everything

One of the most gut-wrenching moments in *The Hero Factor* is a story Jeffrey tells about a staff member who survived the Miracle on the Hudson, the 2009 plane crash where Captain Sully Sullenberger landed a US Airways flight in the Hudson River.

This employee barely made it out alive. He spent 5 hours in the hospital being treated for hypothermia.

And what was the first thing his boss said when he called the office?

"Are you still going to Michigan next week?"

No concern. No empathy. No humanity.

Just business as usual.

That moment, Jeffrey said, was a wake-up call.

Leaders aren't just responsible for profits.

They're responsible for people.

And when you fail at that?

You fail as a leader.

Hard Decisions:
Leadership Is Not a Popularity Contest

Hero leadership isn't soft.

It's not about coddling people.

It's about making the tough calls; but making them the right way.

Jeffrey shared an exercise he does with his team during tough times:

He puts them in a room.

He tells them the company needs to cut costs.

Then he gives them a task: write down names of 8 colleagues to lay off.

Silence. Suddenly, the decision isn't theoretical anymore.

The point?

Leadership isn't about easy choices. It's about real-world impact.

And when people understand the stakes, they engage in the decision-making process at a deeper level.

It's not just about numbers.

It's about responsibility.

Final Thought: Why Hero Leaders Always Win

At the end of the day, The Hero Factor isn't about feel-good leadership.

It's about winning.

Because companies that:

- Put people first
- Lead with values
- Create cultures of trust and ownership

Aren't just better places to work. They're more successful. They attract the best talent. They build stronger brands. They create loyal customers.

So the question isn't *"Should I be a hero leader?"*

The question is *"How long can I afford not to be?"*

Jeffrey Hayzlett's Leadership Playbook
in One Sentence:

> Lead with values, put people first,
> and the profits will follow.

That's The Hero Factor.

That's how real leaders win.

Episode 16:
Purpose leads to Profit

Michael McQueen

Profit Meets Purpose

Michael McQueen doesn't talk about purpose like it's some poster quote in a hallway. He talks about it as a *grid*, a guide for decision-making when pressure hits. Purpose, he says, is what tells you what corners to cut, what costs to wear, and when to stand firm even when it hurts. It's the difference between a brand that folds and one that earns respect.

And it pays.

Purpose-led brands outperform when times get tough. Why? Because they know who they are. They don't just chase metrics. They move from meaning.

When Purpose Shows Up in Practice

Take KFC in the UK. When 80% of stores ran out of chicken, they shut every door, even those that still had stock, because inconsistency violated their core promise. Then they ran a bold full-page apology. No spin. No evasion. Just a cheeky "FCK" on the bucket and a human, accountable tone.

It went viral. Because when a company lives its values, people pay attention.

Closing the Gap Between Lip Service and Culture

Michael doesn't romanticise purpose. He calls out the disconnect when companies say one thing but reward another. When values hang on walls while leaders act on pragmatism. The gap breeds cynicism. The fix? Align incentives with values. Toyota nails this. Sales reps are paid for satisfaction ratings, not just units moved. That's purpose built into the bones of a business.

The Manager's Role: Connecting the Dots

You don't need a company-wide campaign to make purpose real. Michael says a team leader can light that spark in a single meeting. Tell a story. Link someone's work to a broader mission. Create folklore worth repeating. Culture shifts when people *feel* the impact of what they do, when they see that their part matters.

Culture lives in the choices people make when no one is watching. It is not crafted by mission statements but by daily moments of trust, respect, and action. Shape it with purpose, or it will shape you by default.

Episode 157:
Great Monday's Work Culture

Josh Levine

The Culture Question that Changes Everything

Josh Levine was a brand strategist in Silicon Valley when he had an inconvenient realisation: companies are spending millions crafting brand promises they can't deliver internally. The culprit? Culture.

But not culture as window dressing – not beanbags, kombucha on tap or motivational posters – real culture. The kind that lives in the day-to-day decisions people make, in the silent rules teams obey, and in the energy that either fuels trust or chokes it. He defines culture as the *cause and effect of every decision everyone makes.* In other words, culture is the invisible hand, shaping every behaviour in an organisation, consciously or not.

The Cycle of Trust or Tension

Josh points out that culture isn't a thing; it's a system. When someone takes a risk and gets punished, they withdraw. Others see that and shrink too. But when someone picks up extra work for a teammate and gets thanked, it signals a norm. Every act ripples.

This is why psychological safety matters. The tiny "pinches" – sarcasm, passive-aggressive remarks, dismissive eye-rolls – build up.

Not worth mentioning? Maybe. But they chip away at the culture.

One cut at a time. The fix? Start small. Try: *"When you said that, I didn't love how I felt."* It's disarming, honest, and it invites trust instead of conflict.

From Field Guide to Action Plan

Josh Levine's *Great Mondays* isn't a theory book. It's a field manual. Structured around 6 actionable components, Josh offers a toolkit to help organisations not only define culture, but *design* it. There's a reason it's resonating. It shows you how to co-create your culture, not hand it down from above.

For example, his "Values Quick Start" walks teams through crafting values together. Not aspirational fluff, but 3 to 5 behaviours that will move the needle in the next 2 to 3 years. Josh insists on capping values at 5. Why? Because anything more isn't memorable or actionable. Prioritisation isn't just strategic, it's cultural. As he puts it: *"If you have all the values, none of them are true."*

It's Not Just What, It's How

One of Josh's strongest insights comes through his discussion of values-based decision-making. Great cultures empower employees to choose between 2 *viable* options, not between good and evil. Innovation versus efficiency. Risk versus stability. Both can be right. The question is: which aligns with our values right now?

This is where generic values like "accountability" fall flat. If there's no true opposite, then it's not a value. It's a given. Effective values create tension between 2 valid choices. That tension creates clarity.

Recognition that Means Something

Too often, recognition programs celebrate outcomes while ignoring the path taken to get there. The problem? When you reward results without caring how they were achieved, you encourage cutting corners. Josh flips this on its head. He argues for recognising *how* people work, especially when they embody values.

He lays out a 2x2 recognition matrix:

- **Formal from leaders:** Think annual awards, but make them values-aligned.

- **Formal from peers**: Use software or team channels to give public shoutouts, tagged with the value.

- **Informal from peers:** Fun team rituals like passing a silly bacon pillow to whoever best lived a value that week.

- **Informal from leaders**: The underrated power of a coffee chat and a thank you.

Each type matters. Each reinforces the culture you're designing, not just the one you tolerate.

Culture as the Implicit Operating System

The office as we know it is dissolving. Fewer walls, more hybrid teams. Fewer rituals; less cohesion. What takes its place? Culture. Not as a top-down mandate, but as the implicit agreement about how work gets done and how people treat each other.

That's why Josh says culture isn't a soft topic. It's *the* strategy. It's the playbook for every decision when no one is watching. In a world without cubicles or proximity, it might be the only glue that holds your people together.

Final Thoughts

Great Mondays is a guide to building workplaces people don't want to escape from. It's not about perks. It's about principles. If you want a culture that lasts, start with values people co-create. Recognise behaviours that reinforce those values. And never forget: the culture you design is the one you live.

Because what gets tolerated becomes tradition. What gets recognised becomes real.

Culture isn't a mystery. It's a muscle. You just need to train it.

Episode 28:
Deeper Meaning
in Work Experiences

Neil Solomon

UKG: Leading with Purpose and Multipliers

UKG, a global HR and workforce management technology company, head office Boston, is not just a provider of Great Place to Work certification; it lives and breathes the philosophy. In conversations with Neil Solomon, Vice President for Asia Pacific and Latin America, it becomes clear why UKG is repeatedly listed among the world's best workplaces. The secret? It begins with language, behaviour and the belief that leadership is about multiplying, not managing.

The Multiplier Mindset

Inspired by Liz Wiseman's leadership book *Multipliers*, UKG leaders adopt a philosophy that drives 5 times the productivity compared to micromanagement. Multipliers attract, liberate and optimise talent. They invite debate and extend ownership. Instead of diminishing initiative, they unleash it.

As Neil Solomon explains, micromanagers stifle discretionary effort. Multipliers, on the other hand, fuel it. It's a deliberate shift in mindset, embedded into how managers at UKG speak and behave.

Courage to Lead:
A Measure of Management Effectiveness

UKG doesn't just talk culture; it measures it. One of their internal metrics, the Management Effectiveness Index (MEI), asks pointed questions such as: *"Have you had a career development discussion with your manager in the last 6 months?"* The index goes beyond traditional engagement scores. It signals expectations and prompts regular, meaningful check-ins. These metrics are used to coach and support people leaders, not just to judge them. It's part of UKG's philosophy that people don't leave companies; they leave managers.

My Time and the Trust Dividend

Another innovation at UKG is the concept of *My Time*, an unlimited leave policy based on trust. There is no limit to time off, provided employees coordinate with their manager and get the job done. It's a model built on mutual respect and ownership. In fact, leaders often have the opposite conversation with their teams: encouraging people to take time off, recharge, and come back stronger. It's a shift away from presenteeism and toward well-being.

Listening, Reflection, and Emotional Intelligence

Listening is not passive at UKG; it's strategic. It's one of the 5 cultural pillars and perhaps the most human. Leaders are trained to hear not just what is said, but what is meant. Silence is respected. Clarifying questions are encouraged. Neil Solomon admits one of his own leadership growth moments was learning to be comfortable with silence, giving others space to think before speaking. Reflection isn't a side note at UKG. It's a core capability.

From Engagement to Transcendence

In leadership summits, UKG goes beyond strategy to focus on personal growth. One initiative, inspired by psychologist Dr. Scott Barry Kaufman, expanded Maslow's hierarchy of needs into the realm of transcendence. Leaders were encouraged to explore personal fulfilment and purpose, not just professional goals. This is not a retreat from performance. On the contrary, UKG recorded record results while investing in people's inner lives.

People First, Always

Throughout our conversation, one theme kept surfacing: people before profits. UKG leaders write blogs, record 2-minute videos, and stay visible on internal platforms not for vanity, but for connection. Their communication style is human, short, engaging, and real. As Neil Solomon puts it, these touchpoints differentiate from the thousands of emails employees receive. They're moments of clarity and care.

The company's purpose-driven culture shows up in the little things too: flexible schedules, trust-based policies, and mottos that stick. Listening to their teams is not a box-ticking exercise; it's a leadership commitment. And for UKG, that commitment continues to pay dividends, in employee loyalty, customer trust and performance that speaks for itself.

Episode 61:
Leading in Remote Antarctica

Rachael Robertson

Leading in Extremes: Lessons from Antarctica

When Rachael Robertson led a team of 18 people on a year-long expedition to Antarctica, she wasn't just managing operations. She was navigating isolation, 24-hour darkness, and close-quarters tension that could either bind a team or break it apart. What emerged from that experience are 4 profound leadership principles that apply not only to icy outposts, but to boardrooms, building sites, and bustling workplaces everywhere.

Respect Trumps Harmony

One of Rachael's most powerful insights comes from seeing how *artificial harmony* masks dysfunction. Referencing Patrick Lencioni's concept of the 5 Dysfunctions of a Team, Rachael realized that creating a surface-level sense of peace can come at the cost of genuine progress.

"Even if you don't like someone," she said, *"you can still respect their skills, their contribution, and their professionalism. That's what matters."*

Harmony might feel comfortable in the short term. But if it means people are walking on eggshells to avoid real conversations, that comfort is an illusion. Rachael created intentional opportunities for her team to build mutual respect by getting to know what everyone actually did. Not just their job title, but the tasks that kept the expedition running.

For example, when murmurs started circulating about what the plumbers were doing all day, since, in winter, they weren't desalinating water, Rachael invited them to walk everyone through "A day in the life ... " What seemed like a simple team presentation over a spit roast revealed something deeper. When you understand what someone contributes, you're far more likely to value them. It became a strategy she replicated across the team, from the Bureau of Meteorology to the station doctor.

This practice chipped away at the *silo effect*, that creeping sense of "us vs. them" that can form in any organization. When people see the task behind the title, respect replaces resentment. It's a principle backed by research. Rachael noted it's the number 2 motivator, knowing their contribution is recognised.

No Triangles

Rachael introduced a simple but transformative team rule: No Triangles. If you have an issue with someone, you speak directly to them – not to a colleague, not to your boss, and certainly not to everyone excepting the person concerned.

This wasn't just about protecting her time as a leader. (Although she did notice how much energy she regained once she stopped being the unofficial mediator.) It was about empowering her team to handle conflict like adults. She invested 2 months coaching them on how to have these conversations.

Many were tradespeople or scientists, not trained in corporate speak, so she made the communication tools simple and memorable. One such tool was the idea of a language radar. She taught them to tune their ears to emotionally charged words like always, never, everyone, no one. Phrases that trigger defensiveness and cloud the issue.

Instead of saying, "You're always late," the focus shifted to observable facts. "Last week you arrived at 9:00 a.m. We agreed you'd start at 8:30." Factual language reduces friction. It invites accountability without drama.

By refusing to be the go-between, Rachael broke a cycle of dependency and created a culture of ownership. Her team didn't just work together. They learned to work through tension together.

Ladder of Inference

One morning, a plumber came to Rachael and said, *"We need a meeting to decide how to cook the bacon."*

Turns out, the plumbers liked it soft. The diesel mechanics liked it crispy. On the surface, it was a kitchen squabble. But Rachael's curiosity kicked in. She used the "5 Whys" technique to drill down into the issue.

Why was bacon cooking a problem? Because the other team didn't listen. Why don't they listen? Because they throw their tools in the van. Why is that an issue? It creates more work. Why is that a problem? Because it's disrespectful.

And there it was. This wasn't about bacon at all. It was about perceived disrespect.

This is what psychologists call the *ladder of inference*; when we observe someone's behaviour and instantly assign a motive to it. *"They're doing it on purpose to annoy us."* Rachael's team had constructed an entire narrative around bacon based on assumptions. Sound familiar?

The ladder of inference is dangerous because once we climb it, we start treating our assumptions as truth. Rachael's leadership cut through that by challenging the story, not just the symptom. Her approach was clear. Don't let small irritations fester into full-blown conflict. Get curious. Get to the truth. And get back to work.

Silo Effect

Antarctica is the ultimate remote workplace. But even in such tight quarters, silos form. That's why Rachael deliberately created opportunities for cross-team connection.

Hosting "Super Tuesdays," anyone with a hidden talent could teach the group something new. One person taught digital photography. Another gave a talk on living in Prague. Someone ran an Italian language class. It was optional, informal, and wildly popular.

What it did, without forcing it, was build bridges. People began to see each other as more than their job. They saw the whole person. Even if you didn't like someone, you could still say, *"They speak 3 languages. That's impressive."*

Respect grew; silos shrank.

It was a departure from the old "brothers in arms" mentality that had previously defined Antarctic expeditions. Rachael rejected the notion of dying for your teammates. *"We're a federal government workplace,"* she said. *"I won't break a nail for someone else."* That clarity brought structure and realism. It set a new tone. Professionalism with humanity.

Rachael's Antarctic leadership is more than a fascinating story. It's a toolkit. Her lived experience brings hard-won insight into what makes teams work, especially under pressure.

Respect isn't a given. It's built. Conflict isn't toxic. It's inevitable. Silos don't melt on their own. You need to light a fire of connection.

And sometimes, it all starts with bacon.

Rachael Robertson stood at the edge of the world, where silence bites and tempers flare. In Antarctica, culture isn't something you write on a wall; it's something you feel in your bones. Her "No Triangles" rule cuts through the noise, creating a climate of trust in a place where trust could mean survival.

But not all storms howl. Some simmer beneath the surface. Back in everyday workplaces, culture whispers in hallway glances and half-finished sentences.

That's where Steve Simpson listens. He gives form to the unspoken. His concept of Unwritten Ground Rules or UGRs makes the invisible visible, turning culture from an abstract ideal into something we can shape, shift, and lead with intention.

Episode 31:
UGRs, Unwritten Ground Rules

Steve Simpson

UGRs: The Hidden Architecture of Culture

Steve Simpson doesn't talk about culture as an abstract concept. He brings it down to earth with UGRs – Unwritten Ground Rules. Not just another management acronym, UGRs are the invisible norms driving everyday behaviour. They're not written in a handbook or announced at meetings, but everyone knows them. Around here, don't speak up. Around here, new ideas vanish into someone else's credit pile. Around here, silence is safety.

This is the heartbeat of culture; not what leaders say, but what people live. And that's why culture often stays stuck. Because what drives behaviour stays hidden, unspoken. Until someone names it.

Steve names it.

The Business Case for Culture

Steve's research backs it up. Leaders agree that improving culture boosts performance, not marginally, but by 20%, 50%, even 100%. Yet, the problem isn't intent. It's clarity. Culture is overused and underdefined. People nod when they hear the word but struggle to pin it down, which means – nothing changes.

UGRs give culture edges. Tangibility. A way to hold it in your hand and say, *"This right here. This is what's getting in the way."*

From Blind Spots to Culture Shifts

Steve's 5-step process starts with a deceptively simple question: *"What does our culture need to look and feel like for us to be truly successful while making this a great place to work?"*

That's not a values statement stuck on a wall; it's lived clarity. Once the team defines that vision, they uncover the UGRs that contradict it, using sharp, anonymous sentence stems like *"Around here, when someone needs help … "* or *"Around here, when someone offers a new idea … "*

The answers? In Steve's words, *"Gobsmacking!,"* often brutally honest … and honesty is the first lever of change.

Psychological Safety, Power, and Ideas

When new ideas get stolen and repackaged by leaders, that's not initiative; it's emotional theft. It erodes trust. It silences the team. And over time, it kills culture from the inside out.

Psychological safety isn't just about speaking without fear. It's knowing your voice and your contribution won't be hijacked. Tools like Kaizen boards help. But what matters more is the leader's appetite for feedback, their willingness to reflect. And that's what UGRs do. They hold up a mirror.

UGRs aren't just about behaviour. They expose power dynamics, integrity gaps, emotional intelligence. High EQ leaders use them to see what's really going on, then do something about it.

Values, Culture, and the Gap that Matters

Here's the acid test. Ask someone in the business what the company values are. If they need to pull out a document, you've already lost ground.

Steve sees it again and again … value statements that don't reflect reality. UGRs that say, *"We talk improvement"* but the action? *"We steal the credit."* That kind of culture gap breeds cynicism, and eventually, disengagement.

The reverse is also true. When people see ideas acknowledged, whether implemented or not, they keep contributing, culture shifts, results follow.

Profit Through Purpose

Culture isn't soft; it's a profit lever. As Michael McQueen discusses in his episode, purpose-driven companies perform better. UGRs sit right in that continuum.

Get clear on what you want your culture to be. Surface the hidden ground rules. Challenge the ones that hurt. Honour the ones that help. That's not just good leadership, that's strategy.

Because people don't just work for pay; they work for a sense of progress, for meaning, for the satisfaction of being seen and heard. That's why some women keep showing up, even when every dollar they earn goes straight to the cost of child care. It's not about the money. It's about staying in the game, keeping a grip on their identity and not letting the world move on without them.

And that's where the real ROI begins.

Episode 26:
Magnetic Stories

Gabrielle Dolan

Some leaders drop facts like confetti, hoping something sticks. Others? They tell a story. A real one. And when they do, people not only get it, they feel it. Gabrielle Dolan is one of those people.

When Gabrielle was a Senior Manager at one of Australia's top 4 banks, the National Australia Bank, she discovered something important. People remember stories. They lean in. They laugh, they reflect and most of all, they take action.

Making the connection that the most compelling speakers at conferences, whose presentation ideas stayed with you long after, were those who shared stories. The dry presenter spouting just theory and stats, gone; Replaced by leaders who connect on a human level.

Case study: Barbie. Yes, the doll.

Once vilified as a high-heeled, negative role-model of un-attainable beauty standards, Barbie's origin was anything but that. Gabrielle admits at first she dismissed Barbie, never buying one for her daughters. But while researching her book, she uncovered the back story.

Barbie's creator, Ruth Handler, noticed, with the dolls available in the late 1950s, her daughter Barbara could aspire only to be a care-giver. Meanwhile, her son Ken had toys that let him dream bigger.

So Ruth invented the Barbie with adult features and choice of outfits showed girls they can be anything. That doll was a declaration of choice and possibility.

Gabrielle tells us, *"When I heard that story, Nina, it completely changed my opinion of Barbie and the brand. And the story influences my future purchasing decisions."*

That's the power of an origin story.

In Gabrielle's world, that kind of storytelling isn't optional; it's strategic. She outlines 5 types of business stories:

- creation stories (like Barbie)

- culture stories ("touch-the-wall" integrity moments, read on ...)

- customer stories

- community stories

- challenge stories

Each type of story offers a window into what an organisation truly stands for, with authenticity and emotional connection.

One of her favorite workplace stories? A leader sharing how her father, a competitive swimmer, sacrificed a career-defining race because he missed the wall during a turn and chose to go back. He never recovered his position, never made the swim squad, but the story taught his daughter the true meaning of integrity. The leader now tells that story every time a new team member joins. And when tricky ethical decisions arise, staff say, *"This feels like a touch-the-wall moment."* One story, a common language, becomes a cultural compass.

Gabrielle's workshops go beyond the "tell me a story" approach. She pulls teams together from across the org chart and asks questions like, *"Tell me about a time you felt proud to work here"* or *"When did one of your colleagues do something small yet meaningful for a customer?"*

Before long, stories start flowing. One story reminds someone of another, which triggers another. In 2 hours, they might collect 50 stories, and maybe 5 are pure gold. With permission, Gabrielle records them discreetly. Nothing fancy, just a phone app; enough to capture the immediacy of the moment.

And the impact? It's measurable. After storytelling training with Australia Post, the employee engagement score for participants was 13 **percentage** points higher than the rest of the organisation. Not because they got a raise, but because they got reconnected with purpose, with people, with the company's story.

But case studies are not stories, cautions Gabrielle. Stories are real. They happened, and they carry emotional weight. She champions the idea of collecting them into ebooks, videos, even coffee table style printed anthologies. *"Stories,"* she says, *"should be central to onboarding new hires, to illustrating values, and told in team meetings. Teach people the power of storytelling, and you teach them to lead better."*

Her book *Magnetic Stories* shows how to bring a brand to life using this powerful tool. It's not just for marketers; it's for every leader who wants to be remembered.

If your organization isn't capturing its stories, you're not just missing an opportunity, you're missing your legacy.

STRATEGY AND EXECUTION

Episode 95:
The Business Hierarchy of Needs

Jim Gitney

No MBA Required

You don't need a business degree to understand Jim Gitney's Business Hierarchy of Needs. What you need is a burning interest in making your business run better; sharper, leaner, more aligned. And a willingness to ask one critical question: What's the most important goal?

That's where Jim starts. He's not just preaching strategy. He's lived it across 45 years and 200 companies, from GE to Black & Decker to fast-growth startups. And what he's seen, again and again, is the same thing. Most strategies fail not because they're bad, but because they're unaligned. No one talks about the "how," and no one includes the "others" – contractors, contributors, vendors, or customers. Strategy hits a wall, then stalls.

The Framework that Cuts Through Noise

Jim's hierarchy starts at the top:

- Mission
- Vision
- Values
- Leadership traits

From what, to what, by when.

Only then does he introduce the keystone: the most important goal. Not 5 goals. One. Clearly stated. Visible to everyone. From what, to what, by when. Paint it on walls, put it on login screens. Make it inescapable.

Then and only then comes the work: training, tech, structure, hiring, execution. Layered into the system are the "5 Whys," "5 Whats," and "5 Hows" simple diagnostic for alignment. The test is brutal in its elegance: does this task, this role, this project move us toward the goal? If not, kill it. Gitney tells the story of an ice cream machine project that got axed for this reason alone. Cool product, but cold strategy. They weren't in the business of refrigeration. End of story.

Continuous Improvement: Not a Buzzword

Continuous improvement isn't a module to bolt on; it's embedded. But Gitney says most leaders mess this up. They train staff without telling them what to fix. They create improvement teams without constraints. So what happens? The program fizzles. "Flavor of the month," as he calls it.

The fix? Start with thorniest problems. Go to senior leaders. Ask what's in their way. Build improvement projects around those. Progress becomes visible. Energy follows. Momentum builds. That's how a culture of continuous improvement becomes a wildfire and not a flash in the pan.

Why This Matters

Strategy only works if it reaches the people who do the work. That's why Gitney says every person, from the C-Suite to the front line, needs to know the goal and be invited into the "how." That's when alignment becomes more than a poster. It becomes the way people think, decide, lead, and build.

Gitney's pyramid might have 29 elements, but he's clear. You're already doing most of them. The real challenge is this, are they all pulling in the same direction?

Beyond the Blueprint

Jim Gitney gives us the scaffolding – mission, vision, values, the most important goal – all mapped with precision in his Business Hierarchy of Needs.

But strategy doesn't succeed on structure alone. Execution depends on people. And people bring paradox: ambition and insecurity, urgency and avoidance, purpose and politics.

That's why even the most well-designed strategy can quietly unravel. What happens in the boardroom must be lived in the backroom, and that's where Martin Gonzalez turns up the heat, naming the traps that sabotage execution from the inside out.

Episode 132:
The Bonfire Moment
Part 1

Martin Gonzalez

When startups fail, it's rarely the tech that kills them; it's the humans.

Martin Gonzalez, co-author of *The Bonfire Moment*, didn't just observe this; he quantified it. With co-author Joshua Yellin, Martin pored through 360-degree data on more than 900 startup founders and found the similar brutal pattern: 65% of startup failures come down to people issues. Not funding, not product-market fit, but ... people.

And yet, in a world obsessed with blitzscaling and disruption, many founders still treat people skills as optional.

The Four Traps That Set It All Alight

In their book, Martin Gonzalez and Joshua Yellin outline 4 seductive traps that smart, well-meaning founders walk into:

- **Speed**: Moving fast breaks things, including culture. Founders sprint ahead and forget to bring the team with them.

- **Inner Circle**: Founders often hire people who think like them. Sounds great until no one's willing to challenge the boss, and groupthink sets in.

- **Maverick Mindset**: This one stings. Brilliant innovators turn that same disruptive energy toward management, where the rules are different and slower to evolve. They reject hierarchy as outdated bureaucracy. They believe scaling can happen without structure. The result? Chaos disguised as creativity.

Martin lived this firsthand at Google. At one point, the engineering team flattened its org chart completely. Hundreds of staff reported to one VP. No one was approving leave. Feedback collapsed. But out of that came *Project Oxygen*, the landmark study proving that great managers *do* matter. In fact, structure isn't the enemy of innovation, it's what allows innovation to survive.

- **Overconfidence**: The Dunning-Kruger effect is alive and well. The least experienced founders are often the ones most sure of themselves. Ironically, the best ones – the ones who scale – are the most aware of what they don't know. Humility isn't just a virtue; it's a survival skill.

Conflict Is Not the Enemy

Founders who fall into the maverick mindset often chase an ideal of structural harmony and conflict-free growth. But Gonzalez calls that wishful thinking.

There's conflict you need to fix – personality clashes, broken trust.

But there's also **structural conflict**, built into the roles themselves. Sales wants more inventory; operations wants proof of demand. The CEO promises moonshot goals to investors; the CTO worries about tech debt. These aren't problems … they're productive tensions. Trying to erase them flattens the whole system. Great leaders don't eliminate friction; they learn how to ride it.

Lead Like They're Volunteers

The best founders understand one thing – their most talented people have options. You don't "retain" them with a salary. You earn their loyalty by showing how the mission aligns with *their* aspirations. Martin's mantra is simple: **lead like they're volunteers** … because in spirit, they are.

A Playbook for People Who Build Things

The Bonfire Moment isn't just for startup founders. It's a manual for any leader building something new: a team, a division, a movement. The hard truth is, innovation doesn't die from lack of ideas, it dies from leadership that ignores the humans holding the match.

Episode 143:
The Bonfire Moment
Part 2, The Workshop

Martin Gonzalez

After Episode 132 where I spoke with Google's Martin Gonzalez about the concepts in the book, *The Bonfire Moment*, co-authored with Joshua Yellin, I invited him back to the podcast to explore what happens in an actual Bonfire Moment workshop.

The Bonfire Moment Workshop: How to Spark Alignment and Authenticity in One Day

Martin Gonzalez and Joshua Yellin don't run your typical leadership workshop. Their Bonfire Moment event is not about sticky-note platitudes or superficial team bonding. It's a structured, evidence-based intervention that challenges a team's assumptions, surfaces hard truths, and reboots dysfunctional dynamics, in just one day.

From Google to Global

Google's internal team studied over 900 founders and identified the psychological traps that derail leadership. The workshop isn't theoretical. It's a rigorously field-tested process now used by startups and scaleups in over 70 countries, from Latvia to Kenya to Malaysia. Google even certifies facilitators to deliver it.

And it's open source. Anyone can pick up the book, follow the facilitator playbook, and run it. The goal? Democratise deep leadership work.

Why It's Called the Bonfire Moment

It's not a campfire. There's no kumbaya. The bonfire is a metaphor for intensity; the heat of startup life, the pressure of constant execution. This workshop invites teams to step out of the fire together, examine their ways of working, and re-enter with clarity and cohesion.

The Workshop Structure: 4 Blocks of Breakthrough

Each Bonfire Moment workshop is an 8-hour day broken into 4 high-impact blocks:

1. **Face Hard Truths** Participants begin with self-reflection. They fill out a founder effectiveness diagnostic (or 360-degree version), then share in coaching circles. One participant shares a leadership struggle, then turns their chair around to eavesdrop while others problem-solve on their behalf. The shift in posture reduces ego, builds empathy, and unlocks blind spots.

2. **Notice Hidden Dynamics** Each person fills out a "User Guide to Me," answering questions like: Why am I here? What triggers me? How do I want to receive feedback? These guides are shared aloud over a working lunch. It creates a shared understanding of each teammate's quirks, strengths, and edges. And it normalises constructive feedback.

3. **Drop the Masks** This block invites vulnerability. Having already explored how they show up and why, participants are now equipped to speak more freely. The group discusses tensions,

misalignments, and cultural norms that no longer serve them. What is never said but widely felt? That's what gets surfaced.

4. **Resolve Unspoken Issues** Only now, after trust is built and truths are named, do they tackle constructive conversations. It's the crescendo. Conflict doesn't derail the group because they've done the prep work. In many ways, this block writes the new team contract, the implicit agreements going forward.

Why It Works

The Bonfire Moment isn't about surface level tweaks. Just as 19th-century surgeons pivoted from more tools to better hygiene, leaders sometimes have to abandon worn-out practices that no longer serve.

Instead of focusing on flashier tools or bigger goals, this workshop turns inward. What assumptions are driving our leadership style? Are they serving or sabotaging us?

No Fluff, Just Fire

The method is lean and direct. Every exercise is calibrated for depth and clarity. The user guide lives on after the workshop. Teams revisit it when giving feedback, solving tension, or onboarding new members.

If your team is swirling in unspoken frustrations, misaligned values, or psychological drift, you don't need another offsite. You need a Bonfire.

Bring the heat, then do the work.

Episode 75:
Resilience:
It's Not Just Bouncing Back

Jennifer Eggers

The Snicker Test: Getting to Authenticity

Jennifer Eggers doesn't suffer fools ... or fake values.

She tells the story like a slow grin. A health insurance company dripping in "corporate artifacts," slickly laminated values, vision statements hanging like sacred texts in every conference room. They had purpose, they had mission, they had belief systems printed in colored gradients.

But they didn't have truth.

One day, the leadership team was discussing a member's request for a costly lab test. The decision? Let's stall long enough so the patient gives up and pays out of pocket. This, from a company whose wall mantra was *"The member is always right."*

Jennifer couldn't help it. She laughed, and so did everyone else; a smirking, sideways snicker. And that's when it hit her.

The Snicker Test was born.

Having printed out all those artifact posters, laid them across a giant table, and handing each executive a Snickers bar, she instructed, *"Put a candy bar on the value statement that makes you snicker."*

What followed wasn't just cathartic; it was clarifying. Fake stuff got exposed. Hollow mantras got marked. The team began separating what they *said* they believed from what they actually practiced.

When your values make people snicker behind closed doors, you've got a culture credibility gap.

That exercise has become Jennifer's go-to. Not for humiliation, but for liberation. It clears space. It gets leaders aligned around the truths they do live by, and in so doing, it lets go of the lies.

Authenticity isn't just about telling the truth when you feel like it. It's about aligning what you print, say, and do so that your team isn't quietly mocking behind your back the values you hang on the wall. That's a triangle.

The result? Fewer decisions are made in isolation, less political posturing and more clarity on what drives action when no one's watching.

"Alignment," Jennifer says, *"isn't about artificial harmony. It's about naming what's real. Truth over slogans, candour over candy-coating."*

Question ... Is your organisation still holding onto value statements that make your people roll their eyes?

Break out the Snickers.

Episode 88:
Nobody is Smarter
than Everybody

Rod Collins

How to Tap Collective Intelligence

In the old game of business, hierarchy was king. Leaders handed down strategies from on high, and decisions flowed through chains of command. Rod Collins flipped that model on its head.

When Rod was tasked with turning around operations at the $19 billion Blue Cross Blue Shield Federal Employee Program in the United States, he didn't default to top-down strategy. Instead, he pioneered a new kind of meeting, one that treated the group mind as a strategic asset. He called it a Collective Intelligence Workshop. The goal? Shift from positional debate to shared understanding, from siloed voices to integrated decisions.

From Hierarchy to Network

With 39 independent corporations in a business alliance delivering health insurance to 4 million people, alignment was a problem. For 2 decades, closure on critical issues remained elusive.

So Rod asked a different question: what if we stopped trying to lead this as a hierarchy and started treating it like what it truly was – a network? And what if we brought everyone together, not just the usual suspects?

The Setup: Who's in the Room?

Rod and his team designed a 2-day workshop for 40 – 50 participants. Not just senior leaders, but a cross-section of the organisation from all levels, all departments, and all perspectives. With business diversity, cognitive diversity and demographic diversity, it was the whole brain of the organisation in one room.

The rule? No debate. Debate had failed them for years. Instead, they designed a facilitated process that focused on listening, understanding, and co-creating.

The Method: Step-by-Step Collaboration

1. **Clarifying Questions Only**: When someone presented an idea, the only response allowed was a clarifying question; no objections, no pushback. Just an effort to understand. This reset the room's tone from adversarial to curious.

2. **Roundtable Idea Generation**: Participants sat in small groups and generated ideas in response to a framing question like, *"What are the 3 or 4 most important things we need to do to improve this business process?"*

3. **Anonymised Contributions**: Ideas were written on flipcharts and pinned to the wall. Importantly, ideas weren't attributed to individuals. It wasn't "the VP's idea." It is "Table 3's idea."

4. **Distinction, Not Debate**: The next phase was about refinement. Participants compared ideas to identify overlaps or subtle distinctions. The goal was to understand each idea fully enough to say, *"This one is different from that one."*

5. **Condense and Prioritise**: Through discussion, they condensed 30 ideas by half. Then came dot voting. Everyone received sticky dots to allocate

as they wished. Pile all your votes on one item or spread them out.

6. **Synthesis**: The top 4 ideas were usually clear. And remarkably, they often spanned political divides. Idea A satisfied one faction. Idea B, another. Ideas C and D created the glue between them. Together, they formed a high-integrity solution.

7. **Group Ownership**: Because everyone in the room had built it, Rod didn't have to sell the outcome. They left the meeting not just aligned, but proud. And even those outside the room saw the strength of the decision.

Why It Works

In a traditional debate, 2 people argue for their pre-determined positions, often speaking past each other. They listen to disagree, not to understand. At best, the result is compromise.

Rod's approach is the opposite. It begins with understanding. It removes ego. It shifts focus from *"Who is right?"* to *"What do we need?"* It turns meetings into meaning-making.

The Bigger Idea

Rod Collins calls this Collaborative Power. It taps into the natural altruism of human beings when they feel heard and engaged. When the process is inclusive and thoughtful, the outcome is not only more robust, it's also more likely to be implemented without resistance.

And the magic? It's repeatable.

If you want better strategy execution, fewer turf wars, and decisions that stick, don't push harder, facilitate smarter instead. Bring the room together. Ask clarifying questions. Listen with care. Vote with dots. And watch the wisdom emerge.

Episode 140:
What's the Problem
with Meetings?

Nina Sunday and Evan Hackel

Evan Hackel hosts the *Training Unleashed* podcast

I republished on *Manage Self, Lead Others* an episode originally recorded for the *Training Unleashed* podcast with host Evan Hackel.

We explore how to lead meetings that actually work, where action is clarified, participation is equal, and decisions stick I break down exactly why most meetings are dysfunctional and what to do about it.

Why Meetings Fail

First problem? No one considers the experience of the people in the room. No agenda, or it arrives at the last minute. Discussion leaders juggling multiple roles: chairing, note-taking, trying to guide conversation while capturing actions. My advice? Stop multitasking. Assign a proactive minute-taker whose job isn't just to type but to clarify actions: Who will do what, by when.

Phase the Attendance

One of my original game-changing ideas: structure your agenda so everyone attends the top of the meeting, then let people peel away when they're no longer needed. It's a phased attendance model that respects everyone's time. As Evan puts it, *"I've never heard that before ... I like it."*

The Chair, the Leader, the Scribe

Meetings work better when roles are clear. I distinguish 3 roles:

- **Discussion Leader**: The person calling the meeting and guiding topic-specific discussion.

- **Chair**: Not necessarily the most senior. The observer. The timekeeper. The pattern-spotter who makes sure everyone is heard.

- **Minute Taker**: Not a passive scribe. A clarity hunter who follows up when outcomes are vague. This is where Nina's OPUR principle comes in: One Person Ultimately Responsible. Never assign an action to "the team."

AI Minutes? Not So Fast

Evan raises a timely question. *"Can AI take over the minute-taker role?"* My view is, it can assist, but it can't replace human judgment. Let AI record, let humans extract. Use white space, add bullet points, no dense, brick walls of text. And because the forgetting curve is real, write the minutes same-day.

Don't Just List Topics, Define Decisions

Another failing: agendas listing vague topics, side-stepping the question or decision. Instead of *"Should we charge team members for beverages?"* we read on the agenda *"Tea and coffee."* Get specific, get focused.

Case Study: One Dog and Too Much Ego

I share a real-life example of a client whose meetings were all show, no go. The top dog ran the meeting, did the talking, and even took the minutes. Few actions were captured, egos ran unchecked, and no one dared challenge the chaos. My diagnosis? When the meeting becomes one person's monologue, the room disengages. Real power lies in shared ownership.

Addressing the Fear Factor

Evan shares a scenario from a facilitated 3-day strategy session. The CEO is known to retaliate against dissent. My advice? Tread with care. Give feedback in stages. Don't drop the bomb all at once. Ask for permission to share insights, then calibrate based on their openness.

Evan's own approach was smart: Ask the CEO to speak last. Capture ideas anonymously in advance. Share results collectively. Let the ideas speak for themselves, not their authors. Safe space, real talk.

The Compliment That Says It All

Evan sums it up:

"Nina, I have never met a person in my entire life more passionate about effective meetings than you. When I do the pre-work for this training, I ask people questions and you gave me the most elaborate list of ideas and suggestions. You're really an expert on meetings."

One Final Tip

My practical template: every agenda should have a 3-column table:

Topic plus time allocation	Decision required / key points to discuss	Specific participant to contribute

Simple. Smart. Strategic.

Because when meetings are done right, they stop being interruptions and become engines of execution.

PSYCHOLOGICAL SAFETY

Episode 82:
Psychological Safety at Work

Nina Sunday

What Google, Emotional Intelligence, and VW Scandals Teach Us

What is Psychological Safety anyway? Sounds like some soft, HR-fueled buzzword, right?

Wrong.

It's the invisible line between a workplace where people speak up and innovate, and one where they keep their heads down and play it safe (unless the whole thing implodes in a scandal no one saw coming).

Let's start with the basics:

- It's not about mollycoddling people.

- It's not about holding hands and singing Kumbaya in the break room.

- It's about knowing you won't get shot down for speaking up.

It's the difference between a workplace breeding fresh ideas and one that crushes them under the weight of silence.

Google spent years trying to crack the code of what makes a team effective. Is it a manager with tertiary qualifications? Perhaps it is the right mix of personality types, introvert vs. extrovert? Is command-and-control leadership better? Or what about the opposite? Socialising together outside of work? No, none of the usual assumptions fit.

Then, they found the one factor separating effective from ineffective – *psychological safety*. And the 2 attributes that mattered?

- Conversational equality – where everyone in the room has a say.

- Social sensitivity – the ability to read non-verbal microexpressions and body language.

Put these 2 together, and boom! – now you have an effective team.

If either attribute is missing? Get ready for disengagement, group-think, and the kind of boardroom disasters making headlines.

Case Study
Dieselgate: The VW Scandal

Let's talk about how **not** to run a company.

VW. A German powerhouse. Precision. Engineering. A reputation for making cars built like tanks.

And then?

The Emissions Scandal.

A group of engineers discovered they could cheat emissions tests. Instead of raising the red flag, they stayed silent.

Why?

Because VW's leadership had built a culture of command and control, where speaking up wasn't just frowned upon; it could end careers.

Some knew what was happening, knew it was wrong yet didn't say a word.

Millions of diesel cars pumping pollutants into the air. Billions in fines. A global embarrassment.

Why?

Was it because no one felt safe enough to say, *"This is a bad idea?"*

That's the dark side of low psychological safety.

Volkswagen is still navigating the long tail of Dieselgate, while steering toward electric vehicles. But the road toward an electric future is not linear. Adoption rates vary, rivals move fast, and margins stay tight. With each step, they're working to earn back trust and prove transformation is possible.

Here's the lesson: companies killing dissent kill their own future.

The Stimulus-Response Gap

Let's talk about how people lose their cool, and why it's a leadership killer.

Ever fired off an angry email, sent it, and regretted it 5 minutes later?

That's lack of emotional intelligence; inability to hit the pause button before reacting.

Someone with high EQ doesn't react; they *respond*. They create a gap between the stimulus (the trigger) and their reaction.

Sounds easy? It's not. It takes practice.

One trick?

Write the angry email. Wait 6 hours. Realize it is a mistake and delete it. Congratulations. You just avoided a career-limiting disaster.

The 2 Marshmallow Test:
Why Some People Win at Life

Back in the 60s, researchers at Stanford University ran an experiment with children and marshmallows.

The deal was simple:

> *"Here's a marshmallow. Eat it now; or wait and receive another one later. That's 2 marshmallows!"*

Some kids cave instantly. Others stare at the marshmallow like it is a personal demon. They fidget, sing a song, do everything possible to distract themselves to hold out for a bigger reward.

Fast forward 20 years.

Those who delayed gratification had better careers, higher salaries, and more life satisfaction.

Why?

Because self-regulation, the ability to delay knee-jerk reactions, separates high performers from everyone else.

And this applies to leadership too.

Leaders who can't regulate their emotions are volatile. Leaders who think before reacting make better decisions.

Success, in business and in life, often comes down to who can wait for the second marshmallow.

The Art of People Reading

Want to level up your leadership? Learn how to read people.

This isn't some trick, it's about noticing:

> Facial expressions.
> Body language.
> What's NOT being said.

Google's research found the best leaders have a sixth sense for social cues.

Some people are natural pros. They walk into a room and instantly pick up on who's tense, who's checked out, and who's about to drop a game-changing idea.

Others are oblivious. They bulldoze through meetings, missing signs that half the room is seething.

Want to test yourself?

Take Cambridge University's *"Reading the Mind in the Eyes"* test. It's 30 photos, each showing only a close-up of a person's eyes. Your task? Identify the emotion from the 4 words listed around the photo – contemplative, accusing, aghast, nervous, etc.

High scorers are socially sensitive, emotionally intelligent, great leaders.

Low scorers? They miss half the conversation happening right in front of them.

If you want to lead well, train yourself to see microexpressions others miss.

Talking Stick: How to Get to the Truth Faster

Ever sat in a meeting where a few loud fast talkers dominate, while others sit in silence?

That's a team with low psychological safety, where only the confident, extrovert or politically savvy has a say.

One fix? The Talking Stick.

A simple, ancient concept, used by Native American tribes, African councils and even the US Senate stuck in an impasse.

Rule: One at a time, the stick is passed round, and only the person holding the stick speaks.

No interruption.
No dominating.
Everyone gets a turn.

Sounds too simple to work? Yet it does.

In one workplace workshop, I offered a team a twisted, short and thin tree branch as a talking stick. Within minutes, people started holding it like a microphone, realizing, perhaps for the first time, their opinion matters.

Leaders who use this tool unlock insights that perhaps might go unsaid.

The Leadership Lesson You Can't Afford to Ignore

Here's the real takeaway:

Conversational equality isn't just nice; it's essential. Social sensitivity isn't a soft skill; it's a superpower. The best leaders create psychological safety, or they watch their teams wither.

Google figured this out. VW learned it the hard way.
And now?

It's your move.

Want to lead like a pro?

Create space for every voice.
Read the room.
Learn to pause before reacting.

That's how good teams become great.

And that's how you build a workplace where people don't just show up; they show up and they care.

Episode 107:
Bullying: Surprising Myths

Leanne Faraday-Brash

Leanne Faraday-Brash doesn't flinch. As a psychologist, mediator, and author of *Vulture Cultures*, she's spent decades on the frontlines of workplace justice. From investigating grievances to mediating high-stakes breakdowns, she's seen the bruises people carry, invisible but no less painful. In this conversation, she exposes the myths of bullying, the nuance of psychological harm, and what it really takes to lead with fairness and strength in a modern workplace.

What Bullying Really Is

We often think of bullying as blatant aggression – raised voices, slammed doors, public humiliation. But Leanne reminds us that the legal and psychological definition goes deeper. It's repeated, unreasonable behavior creating a risk to someone's physical or psychological health.

That risk doesn't hinge on intent; it hinges on impact.

Even a comment meant as a joke can cross the line if it undermines someone's sense of safety or belonging, especially if it happens more than once. Bullying exists on a continuum. Sometimes it's subtle. Sometimes it's systemic. But always, it's measured by what it does to the person on the receiving end.

The Myth of "You Should've Said Something"

One of the most damaging myths about bullying is that if it were really a problem, the target would have spoken up.

"That's flawed," Leanne says, *"and offensive to most of us."* In fact, placing the burden on the target to confront their bully assumes

psychological safety that may not exist. We can't reasonably expect someone to stand up for themselves in a situation where they feel unsafe. That logic blames the target and protects the behavior.

Leanne encourages people to give feedback with courage, but not obligation. *"You may or may not have realized it,"* is a phrase she coaches her clients to use; a non-accusatory way to assert boundaries and invite accountability. But whether or not the target speaks up, repeated demeaning behavior is still bullying.

Overlap of Bullying and Psychological Safety

Psychological safety isn't just about feeling comfortable. It's about feeling secure enough to take interpersonal risks, to speak up, disagree, offer ideas or challenge the status quo. But what happens when the risk feels too great?

Bullying sits at the far, often unspoken, end of the psychological safety spectrum. It's not just discomfort. It's fear. It's a form of trauma that can rewire the brain, reduce someone's ability to function, and, in the most serious cases, drive them out of the workforce altogether.

Leanne explains that some situations escalate to the point where the targeted person won't enter a room unless a Human Resources or union rep is present. At that point, it's not just about feedback or constructive conversations; it's about survival.

Bullying Doesn't Always Yell

You don't need a raised voice or explicit threat to create harm. Leanne highlights that exclusion, being left out of meetings, social interactions, or decision-making, is one of the most insidious forms of bullying.

Unlike harassment, which requires an active behavior tied to a protected attribute (race, gender, etc.), bullying can occur by doing nothing at all. *"It's not getting in somebody's face,"* Leanne says. *"It's actively isolating and excluding them."* And it's just as damaging.

This form of passive-aggressive behavior often flies under the radar, until the cumulative weight of it breaks someone's confidence.

Performance Management Mistaken for Bullying

Not all discomfort is bullying. Not all friction is abuse. And sometimes, the person feeling slighted is reacting to legitimate, fair feedback. Leanne is careful to draw this line. She's worked with managers who lead with EQ, clarity and compassion, only to have an underperforming team member cry "bullying" in response to a performance review.

Good managers worry about this. The best ones lead with strengths, offer balanced feedback and document everything. *"Reasonable management action taken in a reasonable way,"* she reminds us, *"is not bullying."*

When Bullying Is Real ... and Devastating

Some of Leanne's cases, however, are far from subtle misunderstandings. They are traumatic involving threats, gaslighting, racism, exclusion or humiliation. They leave people broken; not just professionally, but personally. The effects ripple into their home lives, their confidence, their ability to work.

She shares that bullying can alter the brain much like other traumas. It chips away at a person's sense of self. Over time, they second-guess themselves, avoid work, lose interest in hobbies, and fall into depression.

And yes, some perpetrators are aware, but many are not.

Intent vs. Impact

One of the most powerful takeaways from Leanne's insights is this: bullying is determined by impact, not intent. A manager may not realize how their words land. A colleague might think they're being witty, not cruel. But if the result is emotional harm, the behavior must be addressed.

In fact, some people feel genuine distress when they finally understand how much hurt they've caused. They're shocked, embarrassed, and willing to change ... if someone helps them see it.

Role of Emotional Intelligence

Bullying, as Leanne says in her book, is often *"high frustration meeting poor emotional intelligence."* In other words, it's not just about pressure; it's about how we handle pressure.

Leaders who know how to regulate themselves, even under stress, are far less likely to harm their teams. Leanne points to leaders in emergency services and military operations who, under extreme conditions, manage to remain respectful, thoughtful, and clear.

The workplace needs more of them.

How Leaders Can Protect ... and Prevent

So what can leaders do?

- **Create trust and transparency.** People need to know feedback is about growth, not punishment.

- **Lead with strengths.** Start with what's working. It builds safety for what's not.

- **Call out exclusion.** The cold shoulder is as harmful as confrontation.

- **Coach with empathy.** Sometimes people don't know what they don't know.

- **Don't let "tough love" justify cruelty.** High performance can still be kind.

- **Watch for patterns.** Bullying isn't a one-off comment. It's repeated harm.

The Bigger Picture

Workplace culture is moving. What was once tolerated now triggers complaints. That's progress, even if it's messy. In Australia and around the world, organizations are recognizing that belonging isn't a nice-to-have. It's essential.

Leanne Faraday-Brash doesn't sugarcoat it. She's fierce in her defense of dignity at work. Fiercely Australian, fiercely global. And as more of us learn to manage ourselves and lead others, her message has never been more urgent. Trauma has no place at work.

And courage? That belongs everywhere.

Episode 111:
Psychologically Safe Workplaces

Stephan Wiedner

Courage, Confidence, and
the Culture of Psychological Safety

When speaking up is a risk, silence becomes survival.

That's the crux of psychological safety; it's not just about being nice. It's about creating an environment where people bring their full selves to the table and dare to disagree without fear of social sabotage.

This episode featuring psychological safety coach, Stephan Wiedner, unpacks what that really looks like in the wild – in meetings, inside companies that run on conflict-avoidance disguised as harmony.

What It Is, and What It Isn't

Stephan starts by defining psychological safety as a belief, not a policy. It lives in the minds of individuals. It's not a warm-and-fuzzy perk. It's the oxygen of a high-functioning team. And it's not just about the freedom to speak. It's also the belief that when you do, someone will actually hear you.

"It's the courage to speak up and the confidence that what you say will be tended to."

That's the definition Stephan prefers; practical, dual-sided and honest. Amy Edmondson, whose research sparked Google's landmark Project Aristotle, defines it as the belief that a person can take interpersonal risks without fear of negative consequences. Stephan agrees, but adds, it's not just about speaking, it's about being heard.

The Google Backstory: Where It All Took Off

Stephan walks us through the data-rich beginnings of psychological safety's popularity. When Google set out to define the anatomy of effective teams, they tested 250 variables across 180 teams – age, gender, team size, educational background, you name it.

None of these attributes predicted high performance ... until they applied Edmondson's framework.

The result? Psychological safety emerged as the number one differentiator. The other 4 – dependability, clarity, meaning and purpose – all relied on it. Without psychological safety, none of the others stood a chance.

The Hidden Cost of Silence

Psychological safety isn't about managing risk. It's about managing fear, especially the subtle kind; the kind that keeps people from raising a hand, offering a better way or challenging groupthink. That fear doesn't always come from tyrannical bosses. Sometimes it's baked into the team's habits, into unspoken rules about who gets to speak and who gets eye rolls.

"The enemy," says Stephan, *"is apathy."*

Not disengagement, but apathy; the slow-burn decision to lean away instead of leaning in.

Building the Right Habits: "This is How We Do Things Here"

To cultivate psychological safety, managers must make it routine. It's not a policy, it's a pattern. It's reflected in how airtime is distributed, how dissent is handled and how feedback is sought and received.

Reflecting Process

Stephan recommends a technique called "reflecting process." This is where leaders hit pause and call out what's unspoken:

"I'm noticing Jim and Nancy always speak first, and we're not hearing from others. How can we balance the voices in the room?"

It's an invitation, not an accusation. Leaders don't need to solve the imbalance themselves. They just need to name it and ask the team to help restore the balance.

Measuring What Matters

One of Stephan's key contributions is making psychological safety measurable. His firm uses the Psychological Safety Index (PSI), a 7-question survey built on Edmondson's research.

But the data doesn't just spit out a number. It also shows range. If one half of your team scores you at 90 and the other half at 50, your average might look okay, but your culture is still fractured. That variance becomes the launchpad for a deeper conversation.

Episode 128:
Zero Suicide Society

Paul Vittles

Suicide. It's a word that can suck the air out of any room, the unspoken reality that hides beneath polite conversations and cautious smiles. Paul Vittles, who's dedicated his life to dragging this subject from the shadows, puts it bluntly: suicide prevention is one of the great transformational challenges of our time. And the surprising truth? It's actually a happy, hopeful endeavor.

Yes, you read that right. Suicide prevention, according to Vittles, isn't about despair, it's about hope, health, and a fierce belief in life itself. Talking about suicide, openly and directly, isn't part of the problem. It's precisely the solution.

Why We Must Talk About It

Paul sees a fundamental problem is how people flinch away from words like suicide, terrified they'll accidentally plant the idea or offend someone. That's a myth, Paul insists. A dangerous one. *"You don't put ideas into people's heads. If they're suicidal, they're already there. More often than not, they're relieved you asked."*

Here's the unsettling truth. One in 10 people around you have had thoughts of ending their life in the past month alone. *"Now, if you're not supporting those people,"* Paul says directly, *"you're leaving them vulnerable, at risk. Talk to them, and you could save thousands of lives."*

Asking the Unaskable Question

Paul's workshop, starkly titled *Having Difficult Conversations, including the S-Word*, doesn't mince words. *"You must ask direct questions,"* he insists. *"No euphemisms, no dancing around."*

175

It's shockingly straightforward:

"Have you had thoughts of ending your life?"

If yes, then:

"Have you made a plan?"

It's uncomfortable, yes. Terrifying for some. But it's also essential, and life-saving. *"Most people do make a plan, but they reverse it, or hesitate."* he explains. *"You have opportunities, multiple chances, to help keep them safe."*

Paul recalls his early days as a researcher, learning that direct, factual questions bypass resistance. Ask someone their age directly, they might bristle. Phrase it factually, *"What was your age last birthday?,"* they simply answer. Suicide questions are the same. Make them direct, factual, and clear. People respond honestly.

The Detroit Miracle

Paul loves data and frequently highlights the Detroit case study, the Henry Ford Health System, that reduced its suicide rate by 75% in 4 years. In 2009, they achieved the remarkable milestone: 0 suicides.

How did Detroit do it? They didn't wait, didn't rely on bureaucracy, didn't bury their heads in the sand. They asked direct questions, and they asked them earlier, at the first point of contact. It became routine, like checking blood pressure.

Paul's message to workplaces, schools, and doctors is crystal clear: don't wait. Don't send someone spiralling through multiple assessments. Ask early. Ask directly. Save lives.

It's Not Just Mental Health, It's Life

One of Paul's biggest frustrations is the myth that suicide is purely a mental health issue. It's more nuanced, messier than that. *"People can be fine one day, then hit a crisis the next, a lost job, broken* relationship, financial ruin," Paul explains. "These crises trigger suicidal thoughts, often suddenly, even in those with no mental health history."

And here's a chilling reality check: "A CEO is often just 3 months away from crisis, maybe even suicide crisis, because most people live right up to their income. Lose the job, lose the identity, lose hope, it's a rapid downward spiral."

Everyone's Responsibility

Here's the damning statistic Paul wants tattooed onto society's collective conscience: just 6% of the population have received any form of suicide prevention training. That means 94% are wandering around clueless, terrified, avoiding eye contact with this issue.

"Why fight over the 6% who've had training?" Paul challenges. "We need to reach the other 94%. That's our real challenge."

He's right. Suicide prevention isn't a niche topic; it's a societal imperative. Every workplace, every manager, every human with a conscience should take basic suicide prevention training. Like CPR training, standard, essential, lifesaving.

Hope, Not Fear

Paul's vision isn't doom and gloom; far from it. He believes in talking openly, confronting fear directly, and creating a world where no one feels alone. He dreams big, champions bold ambition, and isn't shy about calling out low ambitions as deadly.

In the end, suicide prevention isn't about tiptoeing around tragedy. It's about aggressively, passionately choosing life. It's about looking your colleagues, friends, and family in the eye, asking them honestly, and making sure they know they're not alone.

As Paul says, we're in the hope business now. Let's start acting like it.

INFLUENCE

Episode 27:
Unconscious Bias

Dr Helen Turnbull

Dr Helen Turnbull doesn't tiptoe around the complexity of inclusion. She names it for what it is: work. And serious work at that.

Across decades consulting to global companies, she's identified 3 immutable forces, realities that will never fully disappear, no matter how progressive our workplaces become. First among them: **dominance**. Whether in long-term relationships, boardrooms, or nations, there is always a dominant party. That's not a moral failing. It's a structural reality. But leaders who are serious about inclusion must examine how their own power and privilege shows up. Not in abstract terms, but in how decisions get made, whose voices get heard, and whose don't.

The second immutable force is **unconscious bias**. Dr Turnbull makes it personal. She tells a story of boarding a late-night flight and spotting a female pilot in the cockpit. Her gut reaction? Anxiety. As a consultant in the field, the irony wasn't lost on her. But she realised it wasn't about competence; it was about pattern recognition. Her brain, shaped by years of cultural cues, had coded a "safe pilot" is male, silver-haired, and military-trained. *"I didn't know that bias was there until it surfaced,"* she says. *"But it never really goes away. It just lurks quietly until triggered again."*

Fifteen years later, she flew with another female pilot. This time, she didn't flinch. Progress? Yes. But the bias hadn't vanished. It had simply been spotted earlier, shifted from the back of her neck to her peripheral vision. *"You've got to catch your bias before it opens its mouth,"* she says.

The third immutable force is what she calls **degrees of difference**. We tend to discuss diversity in binary terms: male or female, Black or white, old or young. But within every group, there's variation. Not all women lead the same way. Not all men respond to pressure the same. Dr Turnbull cautions against lazy over-grouping and reminds us that homogeneity is an illusion, even within affinity groups.

So what can we *change*? She identifies **4 permeable forces**, aspects of workplace culture that we *can* shift.

1. **Affinity Bias**: The "mini-me" effect. We tend to favour people who remind us of ourselves, who laugh at the same jokes, share our speech patterns, or hail from familiar backgrounds. That's human. But leaders must ask: *Who am I unconsciously excluding?* Inclusion starts with intentional expansion of who's in the room and whose voice is truly valued.

2. **Assimilation Pressure**: The flip side of affinity bias. Those not in the dominant group often downplay aspects of themselves to "fit in." It's called *covering*. And everyone does it, to a degree. But for marginalised groups, the toll is higher. *"If you're constantly monitoring your accent, your outfit, or your tone to conform, you're not bringing your best self to work,"* she says.

3. **Conversational Inequality**: Fast talkers dominate, quieter contributors are sidelined. Cultural and personality differences widen the gap. One simple fix? *"Go around the room. Invite every voice. It takes only 5 minutes to build trust that lasts,"* says Dr Turnbull. *"When people feel heard, they become more loyal, more present, and more likely to speak up."*

4. **Groupthink Prevention**: Dr Turnbull references corporate disasters where dissenting voices were muted. The lesson? Psychological safety isn't a buzzword. It's a business necessity. Leaders must actively create conditions where risk-averse or contrary views aren't just tolerated, they're welcomed.

Inclusion is layered. It's not just about who's in the building. It's about how they experience being there. Dr Turnbull challenges us to look left and right, not just up and down. To stop asking *"Are we diverse?"* and start asking *"Are we truly inclusive?"*

No check-the-box training or slick mission statement can replace the real work. But if more leaders brought her lens to the table – curious, candid, and unafraid of nuance – we might see that the path to belonging starts not with slogans, but with self-awareness.

Episode 110:
Break that Glass Ceiling!

Linda Fisk

Influence Through Authenticity and Advocacy

Not everyone knows the term "glass ceiling." But they've likely felt it.

Linda Fisk, founder and CEO of LeadHERship Global, defines the glass ceiling as a barrier to upper-level opportunity, one that's often invisible yet unmistakably real. It's the subtle exclusion of women, minorities, and underrepresented communities from advancement. And despite decades of women actively contributing to political, social, and corporate arenas, gender equality in leadership still lags.

Linda's mission through LeadHERship Global is to change that. Her organisation equips women with resources, mentoring, networks, financing, and visibility, whether their goals are TEDx stages, C-Suite or Board positions, or publishing their first book. Whatever their vision of success, Linda helps accelerate it.

Blind Spots and Biases

The episode spotlights how biases, especially implicit ones, hold women back. For example, studies show both male and female hiring managers are twice as likely to hire men over women. Yet when resumes are anonymised, women become up to 45% more likely to be selected. This isn't just a gender issue. Applicants with non-Western names also face unconscious discrimination. Awareness is step one. Policy change, like blind applications and bias training, is step 2.

The Myth of Representation

In many companies where 90% of senior leadership are men, half of those men believe women are already well-represented. One or 2 women in visible roles? That's mistaken for equality. Linda urges leaders to measure, not guess, when it comes to representation.

Tactics for Real Change

- Conduct regular bias and stereotype training.

- Foster a culture of respectful curiosity: *"I don't know, but I'd love to learn."*

- Encourage safe, open conversations across difference.

- Create ERGs (Employee Resource Groups) such as Women's ERGs or Latino ERGs for shared support and collective voice.

Beyond Corporate:
The Glass Ceiling for Entrepreneurs

Linda highlights that even women entrepreneurs face barriers, especially in funding. Female-led ventures are 63% less likely to receive VC funding, despite equal exit success. The ceiling isn't confined to corporate walls.

What Women Can Do

- Build internal and external networks. Industry groups, meetups, and platforms like LinkedIn matter.

- Treat networking as a professional responsibility.

- Educate partners and families that investing time in career development, even just one evening a month, is non-negotiable.

LeadHERship Global: The Mission

Linda's platform offers women a place to:

- Ask the big questions.

- Receive candid, objective advice.

- Get connected with a global network of advocates.

Linda's voice is one of clarity and conviction. This isn't about being louder. It's about being heard. It's about influence, advocacy, and raising the tide for all women.

A Personal Reflection

Years ago I hired a gap year student (between high school and university) to work 4 days a week for a year at my company, Brainpower Training. One of his many responsibilities was occasionally to follow up with prospects over the phone. Because of the unconscious biases present in Australia at the time, I wondered if prospects might assume his call was from an Indian call centre, based solely on his name.

Part of me wrestled with whether I should suggest he use a more Western name while making calls. But to my credit, I never did. It didn't feel right. And how will the world change if I give in to others' unconscious bias?

His voice carried a clear Australian accent. Still, when leaving a message, the only thing prospects might notice was his culturally different name.

I proudly resisted the urge to anglicise his identity. As it turns out, he went on to study medicine and today is an expert on stroke with 9 published papers and hundreds of citations.

Episode 94:
Magic Words that Influence

Tim David

Influence isn't magic, it's science, so Tim David tells us.

From mentalist and magician to authority on the power of connection, Tim's book, *Magic Words*, pulls back the curtain on how subtle shifts in our language can create seismic shifts in outcomes.

If you want to move mountains, you've got to move people first.

Tim shares simple yet potent phrases inviting agreement instead of resistance.

Consider this magic trick. Instead of bluntly asking for help, frame it as, *"Would you be opposed to helping me?"* This clever twist taps into people's instinctive willingness to assist without triggering their automatic defences.

I also favour *"Would you be willing to ... "*

Tim emphasizes the power of indirect questioning; a softer approach that reduces automatic pushback.

Phrases like, *"I'm not sure if you're the right person,"* or *"I was wondering if you could help me out,"* engage people's curiosity and willingness to help, often prompting them to confirm that they are indeed the right person to assist. Drawing on my experience with Neuro-linguistic Programming, I mastered the art of asking a question without directly asking it.

> *I don't know if ...*
> *I'm wondering if ...*

This construction removes the weight of direct questioning and feels less interrogative, inviting more genuine responses.

And then there's the persuasive heavyweight: "because." Our brains are hardwired to crave reasons, and the magic is in repeating it. *"We need this done because ... because ... because... "* stacks your odds, nudging even skeptical minds toward yes.

Tim dissects the underestimated power of "but." Known as the "but eraser," it wipes out whatever came before it, elevating whatever follows. So swap the criticism sandwich: *"You did great, but ... "* for *"There's one thing to address, but overall you nailed it."* Suddenly, feedback feels empowering, not punishing.

He introduces the "but reversal," a powerful technique that reframes a negative response into something positive. If someone declines your request saying, *"I'd love to, but I can't,"* flip it around to, *"I can't right now, but I'd love to."* It changes the emotional memory of the conversation.

Then there's the magic word "if," which gently bypasses resistance. When someone insists they can't do something, Tim advises to respond with, *"I know it feels like you can't right now, but what would happen if you could?"* This simple tweak opens possibilities and encourages creative problem-solving.

Tim's journey from magician to communication expert emerged from years of live experimentation. Changing even one word in his performances led to dramatically different reactions, highlighting the potent, hidden power of language.

These aren't mere tricks; they're neuroscience-based shortcuts. The human brain loves efficiency, often taking mental shortcuts when processing information. Words like "because," "but," and "if" tap directly into these shortcuts, making intentional communication highly effective.

Because at the end of the day, as Tim vividly illustrates, whether resolving hostage crises with genuine gratitude or fundraising millions with the right framing, real magic happens when we speak intentionally.

Episode 63:
Yes, And ...

Avish Parashar

Yes, and ...
The Power Move that Builds Influence

Right out of the gate, Avish Parashar doesn't tell. He shows. He starts with a roleplay. Just a simple decision-making scene about where to meet for lunch. And like a knife through warm butter, the impact slices through the noise.

You hear *"Yes, but ... "* and it grates. Each polite deflection is like a pinprick to the soul. The suggestion lands, but instead of a lift, you get a tiny vacuum of resistance.

The "Yes, But ... " Spiral

A simple question: where should we meet? A simple answer: a cafe at the Sydney Opera House. And then: "Yes, but it's touristy." Then again: "Yes, but I want real food." And again: "Yes, but it sounds too fancy."

By the end of the spiral, you want to close your laptop and move to a different city. The enthusiasm? Bled out, one pinprick at a time.

Enter: "Yes, And ... "

Rewind. Same question. Same answer. But this time:

> *"Yes, and since I'm new here, I trust your judgment."*

> *"Yes, and it sounds like a great way to experience something iconic."*

> *"Yes, and I love that it offers variety."*

189

I can feel the shift. Even during a podcast Zoom call, our energy rises, excitement brews, connection solidifies.

Why It Works

"Yes, but ... " is polite rejection. It's argument with a smile on its face. It negates everything said before the word "but."

"Yes, and" is invitation. Collaboration. Possibility. It's Tim David's but eraser.

Avish says it best: *"Yes, but ... is negative. It's an argument. It stops all progress. Yes, and ... is positive. It builds energy, makes fresh suggestions, creates movement."*

In the Workplace: A Tactical Reframe

Here's the scenario. You're a manager. An idea is floated.

- *Yes, but we're too busy.*
- *Yes, but we tried that already.*
- *Yes, but that's not how we do things.*

You may as well say, "No, thanks," with a velvet glove. But reframe it as:

- *Yes, and let's look at timing.*
- *Yes, and maybe we can adopt it this time.*
- *Yes, and let's explore how we could make that work here.*

It's not semantics. It's strategy.

The Trigger Word Nobody Likes

Want to know what derails trust fast? *"Unfortunately ... "*

As in:

- *"Yes, but unfortunately, you didn't follow the policy."*
- *"Yes, but unfortunately, we can't help you."*

The moment *"but unfortunately"* lands, your customer or colleague stops listening. It's code for: this is going nowhere. Avish calls it a trigger. He's right.

It's Not Just Wordplay. It's Mindset

Avish warns, people sometimes swap in "Yes, and ... " but keep the same resistant tone: *"Yes, and I don't want to do that."* Nice try. Real power comes from shifting attitude, not just vocabulary.

"Yes, and ... " asks you to park your defensiveness; to open to uncertainty, to risk exploring new territory.

Fear and the Yes, But ... Reflex

Why does the world lean on "Yes, but ... " like a crutch? Answer: because it feels safe.

- Safe from change.
- Safe from being wrong.
- Safe from admitting someone else had a better idea.

It's comfort-zone language; while growth, influence, live outside that zone.

This is about real connection. About staying open. About being more human.

Avish's improv background makes him the perfect messenger. In improv, "Yes, and ... " keeps the scene alive. In leadership, it keeps possibility alive.

Try it next time you're tempted to shoot something down. Pause. Rethink. Say yes. Then build on it.

Because influence isn't just about having answers. It's about keeping the story going.

APPRECIATION

Episode 120:
Leaders Showing Appreciation

Avi Liran

The Power of Appreciation

It's not a perk. It's not some HR initiative tucked between an uninspired annual review and the polite fiction of a "team-building retreat." No, appreciation is the oil that keeps the engine from seizing up. It's the difference between a workplace that hums and one that drains the life out of people.

Avi Liran, self-proclaimed "Chief Delighting Officer," works with many Fortune 500 companies to create delightful employee and customer experience. Turns out, most leaders get it completely wrong. Five levels of appreciation, 5 ways to move past a hollow "good job" and into something that actually fuels people.

The First Mistake: Following the Golden Rule

You might know that saying, *"Treat others how you want to be treated"?* It sounds noble, but often misses the point. Because what you want — and what they want — are rarely the same thing. Avi calls this the "peanut butter problem." You love peanut butter, and you buy your friend the world's best peanut butter. Turns out, they're allergic to peanuts. What was meant as a thoughtful gesture is actually a mishap.

Leaders do this all the time. They assume what they appreciate is universal. The best leaders don't make that mistake. They listen. They get into the trenches, they observe, they learn what actually makes their people tick. Then, and only then, do they start showing appreciation in a way that lands.

Level 1: Fix What's Broken

You know what drains motivation? Pointless irritation. Picture this. Your team works hard to serve customers, but there's a recurring issue that keeps making their job harder.

It's fixable, they flag it, management nods, smiles ... but does nothing. And so, the cycle continues.

Avi calls it 'fix it fast', because appreciation starts with action. If you're a leader, here's a hard truth. Ignoring persistent problems is a direct signal you don't value your team members. Fix what's broken, show them you're paying attention, and watch engagement skyrocket.

Level 2: Learn What Delights, Then Surprise Them

Predictability is great for payroll. Appreciation? It thrives in the unexpected. The best customer experiences don't start with the customer. They start with your team members. What makes them light up? What keeps them invested?

Leaders who figure this out don't just get higher retention, they get people who actually care.

Avi's method? Walk and talk. Literally. He invites employees to join him on morning walks, just talking. One of his interns, Brian, had a dream of being an F1 (Formula 1 driver. He had no money, no connections, just raw passion. Avi didn't just listen, he moved. He connected Brian with a racing team, and a few months later, the kid was out there winning.

That's leadership. That's appreciation. Not a half-hearted *"I see you,"* but a full-throttle *"I get you and I'm in your corner."*

Level 3: Elevate

Pride – Show the Impact

Indra Nooyi, former CEO of PepsiCo, wasn't interested in generic pats on the back. When she took the helm, she didn't just thank her top executives. She went straight to their parents. She handwrote letters – real, ink-on-paper letters – telling them how much their child had impacted the company.

One exec's dad was so moved he made copies and handed them out to the neighbors. The result? Parents overflowing with pride, leaders feeling deeply valued, and the workplace buzzing with renewed loyalty and purpose.

Level 4: Ritualize Appreciation

If appreciation is only an occasional "well done" at the annual town hall, you're doing it wrong. It needs to be baked into your culture.

During the turbulence of the dot-com crash and the aftermath of 9/11, hotelier, Chip Conley, found himself leading a team who were emotionally and financially shaken. With occupancy rates plummeting and fear in the air, he realized spreadsheets weren't going to lift spirits, but stories might.

Every leadership meeting was to start with a story of appreciation. Not numbers, not strategy, but stories! Team members sharing positive stories, acts of kindness, or moments of resilience.

For example the story of Billy the bellboy, who ran up and down 10 flights of stairs when the elevator was broken. Leaders didn't just acknowledge it, they celebrated it, sent a senior exec to personally thank him, and gave him a free stay at another property.

This simple shift turned panic into purpose. As hope became part of the daily agenda, morale rose, and his team weathered the storm, not just intact, but inspired. In a dark times, it was the light of appreciation that kept them going.

Avi's lesson here? If you want appreciation to stick, make it a habit, embed it into company culture, not add it as an afterthought.

My Own Experiment with Appreciation

One year I ran my own appreciation experiment with my team at Brainpower Training. It was a pre-Christmas lunch, 6 of us around a restaurant table, I handed out 6 different-colored sheets of paper, each with the start of a sentence printed at the top:

One thing I appreciate about [name] is: _____

One by one, we passed each appreciation sheet around, each of us completing the sentence by writing something we genuinely appreciated about the individual named.

By the end, everyone had a full sheet of personal compliments from their peers. My office manager kept hers taped on the wall behind her desk for years, through two office moves. Because that's the kind of thing that matters.

The Takeaway: Make It Stick

Leadership isn't a title. It's an impact. And impact isn't built on perks and salary. It's built on appreciation. Real, raw, no-padding appreciation that tells people, they matter.

Avi Liran's levels of appreciation aren't a gimmick. They're a blueprint.

The question is, are you the kind of leader who just says "thanks," or the kind who makes them feel appreciated.

Episode 93:
Passion @ Work

Shivani Gupta

Appreciation:
Passions, Presence and a Nepalese Boy

Shivani Gupta started out ticking all the boxes. Engineer, MBA, a rising star in the corporate galaxy. By the age of 30, Shivani Gupta had climbed the rungs of a global career ladder that many only dream of.

But it took a single, unexpected moment in a remote Nepalese village, seated under a tree, for her to realize she was living the wrong story.

The moment wasn't loud. It didn't involve a standing ovation or a pay rise. It was a boy. A 5-year-old with bright eyes, running towards her, excited. He knew she carried sweets. She gave him one. He bit it in half, gave the other piece to his little sister, and wrapped up the rest for later. No demands. Just instinctive generosity.

Shivani sat and wept. She had everything yet was unhappy. This boy had nothing yet radiated joy. That was the spark. Within a week, she resigned from her senior job, ended an unfulfilling relationship and committed to a new path: helping people find meaning, success and most of all – joy. Not the temporary sugar rush of external wins, but the kind that runs deep and lasts.

In our conversation, we talked about the weight leaders carry. "Exhaustion" came up more than once, a word Shivani says surfaces repeatedly in global surveys of leaders and managers. Everyone's been giving and giving, to their team, to their families, to their companies. But the tank is empty. Resilience is wearing thin.

So how do you keep the lights on, inside, when everything around you keeps asking for more?

Shivani's answer is equal parts strategy and soul.

Managers, she says, must learn to identify and feed the passions of their people. Stop expecting everyone to be like you. Some of your best team members might value family more than work. Others might live for their morning run or their creative side hustle. If you want them to stay, and thrive, meet them where they are. One of her team worked 4 days a week to prioritise family. Another received a paid gym membership to support their fitness goals. Each one performed better when their personal priorities were respected.

But it doesn't stop with perks. Leaders need to be attuned to mental health warning signs – absenteeism, presenteeism, low energy, emotional flatness. Shivani urges workplaces to provide tools, not just platitudes. A mindfulness space, journaling, financial literacy sessions, even introducing a "one-word check-in" at the start of meetings, just a word to express how someone feels is uplifting. If you can provide a chart of 150+ feeling words, it helps team members go beyond "fine" or "busy."

Her 10-10-10 formula is a practice in presence:

- 10 minutes of journaling
- 10 of reading
- 10 of meditation

Add a minimum 30 minutes of movement – walking, stretching, yoga – and you've got a foundation for self-leadership and joy. Not the performative kind, but the sustaining, steady kind that makes bad days survivable and good ones intentional.

Episode 62:
Joy in the Workplace

Sheryl Lynn

Dan Silberberg reminded us that presence and wisdom walk hand in hand. And when leaders cultivate both, people feel held. Not handled.

Then along comes Sheryl Lynn. Her approach to appreciation is sensory, embodied, and anchored in stillness. She calls it the Chair of Joy.

Joy Versus Happiness: A Deeper Current

Sheryl Lynn makes a clear distinction between fleeting happiness and enduring joy. Happiness, she says, is a sugar hit like an ice cream cone or the new car smell. Joy is different. Joy roots itself in the nervous system, builds resilience, and sustains us through hardship. And that's what makes it a leadership priority. Because how do we expect people to show up with energy, optimism and care if they never pause to notice what brings them joy?

A Catalyst for Connection

Sheryl's physical Chair of Joy – white leather, gold trim, diamond studs – travels with her to conferences and corporate offices, inviting people to sit, slow down, and reconnect.

But any chair can be a Chair of Joy – a garden bench, a quiet nook by the window. Power lies in what happens while sitting there.

In our conversation, I asked Sheryl what she sees when leaders adopt the Chair of Joy process across their teams. Her answer?

People start seeing each other. Really seeing each other. Walls come down. Conversations become more human. That's where appreciation begins, with attention.

The Experience: A Pause, A Breath, A Memory

Sheryl guided me through a Chair of Joy experience during the podcast. It began with locating a physical space in my home that feels comforting and grounded. For me, it was my front patio. A chair beside a glass table. Surrounded by greenery and birdsong. I realized I used it only once a day. By end of our conversation, I'd already decided to sit there for every tea break.

Next, she asked me to close my eyes and recall a deeply joyful moment. The first memory that came was receiving my acceptance confirmation to study at the Australian Film, Television and Radio School; a career-defining moment. I cried with joy that day. The second memory was playing fiddle in a country rock band and winning Best Instrumentalist. Another moment of triumph.

These weren't random flashbacks. They were windows into how I expressed creativity, a core source of joy in my life. That's the magic of the Chair of Joy process. It reconnects you with what lights you up, either from the past or in the present.

The Language of Joy at Work

Sheryl points out that our language often sabotages joy. Words like need, should, must, and have to feel heavy, even transactional. Leaders can instead use the language of possibility: *I would love to …, I feel inspired by …, I wonder if …* That shift matters. Language shapes how people feel, and how they feel affects how they perform.

Joy-based leadership isn't about singing kumbaya in the break room. It's about retaining your best people. It's about bringing oxygen back into burned-out teams. It's about tapping into purpose, even when budgets are tight and deadlines are real.

The Chair of Joy Experience
(Step by Step)

1. **Find your Chair of Joy.** This is a physical chair where you feel grounded. Ideally a peaceful space where you won't be interrupted. It could be at home, at work, or outdoors.

2. **Anchor with your senses.** Sit comfortably with feet flat on the floor. What do you see, hear, and feel? Let your senses tune in.

3. **Take a deep breath.** Breathe in for 6 counts. Hold for 6. Exhale slowly for 6.

4. **Recall a joyful memory.** Let your mind bring up a time when you felt joyful. Let that moment replay in your body. What were you doing? Who was there? Let yourself relive it.

5. **Repeat with a second memory.** After another breath, allow another joyful moment to emerge.

6. **Name the emotion.** What one word describes the feeling those memories give you?

7. **Visualize a container.** Place that feeling word into a mental container. It could be a jar, a box, a vessel – something that stores and protects the essence of that joy.

8. **Carry it forward.** Ask yourself: how can I bring this energy into today? Into the next meeting? Into how I lead?

You can revisit this process daily, even for a few minutes. Over time, it becomes a habit of renewal; an anchor for leadership energy, resilience, and appreciation.

Sheryl's Chair of Joy experience is more than a wellbeing tool. It's a mindset, a ritual, and a reminder that joy is not the reward; it's the fuel.

PERSONAL BRANDING

Episode 34:
Executive Presence:
How to Build It

Pamela Wigglesworth

You know it when you see it. Executive presence is that elusive, magnetic force field we can't quite define, but we remember it.

Some people call it poise, rizz, gravitas, the it-factor.

And the best leaders? People don't just listen to them. They lean in.

Pamela Wigglesworth, in episode 34 of the *Manage Self, Lead Others* podcast, calls it the *"je ne sais quoi."*

Many professionals are blind to the silent signals they're sending. Their voice says, "I'm prepared." But in a virtual meeting, their echoey sound (because they're not using a proper mic), their hazy camera image (because they're not using a webcam), their indistinct facial expression (because there's a window behind them causing background over exposure, making their face a silhouette), and camera angle is low to high, (because they didn't use a laptop stand to align the camera in a direct line to their eyes).

Guess which message sticks?

Pamela works with C-Suite execs, polishing their presence until their message sings.

Not louder. Clearer.

Not flashier. Sharper.

Her point is brutal and brilliant: it's not what you say that carries weight. It's how you show up before you open your mouth.

Gravitas.

Communication.

Appearance.

That's the holy trinity of executive presence. You could be spinning gold in your brain, but if your shoulders slump and your energy drips off the screen like day-old coffee, your credibility goes with it.

And let's be clear. Virtual isn't a pass. In fact, it ups the ante.

On-screen, you're flattened to a head-and-shoulders square. Every twitch, blink, and awkward slouch is magnified. It's not a Zoom or Teams call. It's a stage, and you're the show.

So here's the hit list, straight no chaser:

- **Camera at eye level.** Prop it up with printer paper, books, whatever. Nobody wants to see your ceiling fan or your nostrils.

- **Lighting from the front.** Not behind. Not beside. Front. Always.

- **Clothing that respects the moment.** Wear the t-shirt on your own time. Keep a jacket nearby. Toss on a scarf if you need a quick upgrade.

- **Energy matters.** The vibe you bring to the first 60 seconds lingers like cheap aftershave. Be intentional.

And for the love of all things caffeinated, stop eating on camera. We see you. The webcam sees everything.

Let's talk about nerves.

Everyone gets them. Yes, even the ones who look born for the spotlight. Executive presence doesn't mean you're immune to fear. It means you've learned to dance with it.

Pamela tells her clients to use that nervous energy as fuel. Breathe deep. Plant your feet. Talk to the dot like it owes you money.

The more you show up, the more it fades. Courage isn't the absence of nerves. It's deciding to speak anyway.

Presence is not about perfection. It's about signal. Pamela says, *"What's the silent narrative you're sending before you speak?"* That question is jet fuel. Pour it on everything. Your meetings. Your pitches. Your leadership.

Want influence? Start before you open your mouth. The camera's already rolling.

> *Your voice and your content are your superpower.*
> —Pamela Wigglesworth

"Don't dress for the job you have. Dress for the message you want to send."

This isn't a game of dress-up. It's about respect. For yourself, for others, and for the work you claim to care about. And if you think it doesn't matter? Well, someone else just showed up looking ready, sounding ready, being ready.

Guess who they're going to follow?

Episode 126:
Your Unique X-Factor

Yamini Naidu

Standing Out by Standing True

When you hear Educator of the Year, Yamini Naidu, speak, something shifts. Not because she commands attention (she does), or because she's mastered the fine art of storytelling (she has), but because she slices through fluff and delivers truth with elegance. Yamini's superpower? Helping others crystallise their personal brand in just 3 words.

A decade ago, this might've sounded gimmicky. Today, it's non-negotiable. In a distracted world, clarity is currency. And Yamini's framework delivers.

Your Three-Word Brand: The Why and the How

Yamini doesn't teach people to invent traits. She draws them out, excavating essence. She guides you to find the real, the resonant, and the relevant. Her signature process is more than a catchy exercise. It's a mirror.

She often begins with the uncomfortable: what are 3 *negative* words people might use behind your back? It's confronting, yes. But illuminating. Because from the shadow emerges shape. And from shape, authenticity.

Then, you pivot. What 3 words describe you at your best? Not what your resumé claims. Not what your job title demands. But you, when you're in flow. In leadership. In alignment.

The Brand You Already Are

This isn't about reinvention. It's about revelation. Yamini's brilliance lies in helping people recognise what others already see. You're not creating a brand. You're claiming it.

She says, the gold standard is this: if you left the room, and someone asked your team to describe you in 3 words, would their answer match yours? If it doesn't, you're either performing or hiding. Either way, there's misalignment.

Making It Memorable

Your 3 words must land. They need to be distinct, not bland. Confident, not arrogant. Evocative, not try-hard.

Take me, Nina Sunday. Yamini distilled mine to this: *Curator of conversations, swimmer with dolphins, speed reading trailblazer.*

It's a living description. It captures the essence of my podcast, my kinship with cetaceans, and that in my lifetime I helped more than 100,000 people unlock speed reading as a true superpower.

And importantly, it's how I want to show up. Yamini's process makes that clarity possible.

Not About Ego, About Echo

This isn't personal branding as a flex. It's resonance. When you name your essence, others remember. You become easier to introduce, easier to refer, easier to trust.

Because branding isn't what you say about yourself. It's what people say when you're not in the room.

The Yamini Effect

Yamini doesn't shout. She doesn't need to. She helps leaders and teams get crystal clear on who they are, what they stand for, and how to convey that in 3 memorable, true-to-you words.

It's deceptively simple. Quietly powerful. And like all things that last, it's built on truth.

If you're struggling to define your brand, you don't need a new website or a tagline. You need Yamini.

Because in a world of noise, the clearest signal wins.

MOTIVATION

Understanding Your Explanatory Style and Why It Matters

What story do you tell yourself when things go wrong?

For optimists, setbacks are speedbumps. For pessimists, they're proof. Proof that they're not good enough. Not lucky enough. Not meant for more.

In this chapter, we explore the work of psychologist Martin Seligman's *Learned Optimism* and his theory of explanatory style, the way we explain good or bad events to ourselves. Optimism and pessimism aren't just vibes, they're mental habits. Patterns. Predictors of resilience, motivation, even physical health.

> Optimists don't just "stay positive."
> They reframe.
> They say: "This didn't work out, but it will."

We explore the workplace impact of both mindsets, unpack how they show up in relationships, and link optimism directly to goal-setting, adaptability and overall wellbeing. You'll also discover how even the most self-aware among us can be triggered into pessimism without realising it, and how to interrupt those thought loops.

And then comes your moment: a **10-question self-assessment** to reveal your current mindset and where it might be holding you back. Optimism can be trained, just like any muscle.

Optimism is the ultimate performance enhancer, and it's not something you fake. It's something you build.

So before we head into vision boards, bucket lists, and big, audacious asks ... let's check in. Let's get honest.

Let's Find Out:
What's the Story You're Telling Yourself?

Self-Test: How Optimistic Are You?

Use this 10-question self-assessment to identify your current mind-set and explanatory style. Choose the answer that most closely reflects how you typically think.

1. **You applied for a job but did not get an interview.**

    A)   Maybe I'm not the kind of candidate employers want.

    B)   This company is not the right fit for me.

2. **A close friend cancels plans at the last minute.**

    A)   They don't really value our friendship.

    B)   They must be really busy today; we'll reschedule soon.

3. **You made a mistake on an important work project.**

    A)   I always mess things up; I'm just not competent.

    B)   I made a mistake, but mistakes are part of learning.

4. **You've been trying to improve your fitness but haven't seen results yet.**

    A)   This routine isn't giving me the results I expected; I'll adjust my approach.

    B)   I'll never be fit, no matter what I do.

5. **A romantic relationship ends unexpectedly.**

    A)   Relationships just never work out for me.

    B)   This one didn't work, but I'll find a better match in the future.

6. **You receive unexpected praise from your manager.**

    A)   I must have gotten lucky this time.

    B)   I worked hard, and my efforts paid off.

7. **You set a big personal goal, but progress is slow.**

   A) It's taking longer than expected, but I'll keep going and adjust if needed.

   B) I doubt I'll succeed, so maybe I should stop trying.

8. **A colleague is praised for an idea you contributed to.**

   A) They always take credit. This keeps happening.

   B) I'm glad the idea was recognized. Next time, I'll highlight my contribution.

9. **Your manager assigns you a challenging new project.**

   A) This is overwhelming. I'm probably not capable of handling it.

   B) This is a great opportunity to grow and prove myself.

10. **A company-wide change affects your workflow.**

    A) Just another disruption that will make everything harder.

    B) Change is part of work. I'll adapt and find the best way forward.

Scoring

Optimistic responses:

1B, 2B, 3B, 4A, 5B, 6B, 7A, 8B, 9B, 10B

Pessimistic responses:

1A, 2A, 3A, 4B, 5A, 6A, 7B, 8A, 9A, 10A

Interpret Your Score

- **Mostly Optimistic Answers**
  You have a strong, growth-oriented mindset. You see setbacks as temporary, and you believe in your ability to adapt, learn, and move forward.

- **Mixed Answers**
  You're generally optimistic but may have blind spots or recurring doubts in certain areas. With awareness and practice, you can shift toward a more resilient and constructive mindset.

- **Mostly Pessimistic Answers**
  You may default to caution or negative thinking, but optimism is a skill, not a fixed trait. By examining your automatic thoughts and actively reframing challenges, you can train your brain to expect better outcomes.

Motivation:
The Power of Certainty

If leadership is about driving results through others, then motivation is the fuel that powers every decision, every action, every leap of faith. And while we often treat motivation as something fleeting, like a spark that comes and goes, the truth is, certainty sustains motivation far longer than inspiration ever could.

This final chapter explores motivation from multiple angles: the science of why we act, the emotional energy that either fuels us or drains us, and the powerful role that belief – yes, even bold belief – plays in creating momentum.

We begin with **Helle Bundgaard**, who breaks down the neuroscience of motivation into 4 building blocks: energy, needs, talents, and purpose. She reveals that most people are already motivated. What holds them back is what gets in the way. The drainers, the disconnects, the emotional triggers left unexplored. Her hierarchy of motivation gives managers a language to have deeper conversations, ones that lead to clarity and confidence.

Next, we revisit Victor Vroom's Expectancy Theory, which reminds us that motivation isn't magic, it's math. People are driven when they believe their effort leads to performance, performance leads to rewards, and the rewards meet a meaningful personal need. In short: certainty creates motion.

Then we shift gears into practice.

We explore the power of the **vision board**: a tangible, visual way to hardwire intention, cultivate expectancy, and remind yourself daily of what you're moving toward. We follow with **Trav Bell**, the Bucket List Guy, whose message is clear: Don't just plan your work. Plan your life.

And finally, we close with Mark Victor Hansen, co-author of Chicken Soup for the Soul and Ask! His story weaves motivation with manifestation. He shows us what happens when you ask for what you want, not once, but repeatedly, with faith, with conviction, with certainty. Act as if the universe is already rearranging itself in your favour.

Whether you're data-driven or spiritually inclined, this chapter offers one final truth:

Motivation lives at the intersection of belief and behavior. And certainty, earned or chosen, is what keeps you moving when the path ahead gets foggy.

Episode 67:
What Motivates People

Helle Bundgaard

Cracking the Code of Motivation

Motivation isn't a fluffy HR concept. It's the engine behind every choice we make. And if you're leading people, you'd better know what fuels their fire ... and what drains it.

In this episode, Motivation Factor founder Helle Bundgaard takes us beyond Maslow and Daniel Pink into a more nuanced, neuroscience-backed framework for understanding what makes people tick at work. Her *Hierarchy of Motivation* – energy, needs, talents, and purpose – offers a lens for conversations that go deeper than goal-setting. It's not just about lighting people up. It's about knowing what quietly switches them off.

"You can't motivate people unless they're motivated to be motivated."

Helle reframes motivation as dynamic, personal, and situational. She shows us how overused talents, unmet needs, and emotional triggers can sabotage even the most intrinsically motivated team members, and how getting rid of energy drains can be more powerful than adding new perks.

This isn't a one-size-fits-all solution. It's not even about keeping people "highly motivated" 24/7. It's about helping them stay in alignment with what matters and giving managers the language to guide that process.

Motivation, it turns out, isn't just about passion or purpose. It's about creating enough certainty through clarity, alignment, and honest reflection that people feel safe to step into stretch zones, shift with change, while still staying true to themselves.

Before you can lead others, you have to believe your effort makes a difference.

That's where Vroom's Law of Expectancy comes in.

Victor Vroom suggested the relationship between people's behavior at work and their goals isn't as linear as once believed. Motivation, he proposed, is a function of 3 things:

- The belief that effort leads to performance,

- That performance is rewarded,

- And that the reward satisfies a deep personal need.

In other words, people are most motivated when they have certainty the effort is worth it.

Vision Boards and the Power of Positive Expectancy

A couple of years ago I attended a workshop on creating a vision board, (although it wasn't the first I'd ever created). What made this one special was the group setting: the facilitator brought along a stack of magazines and scissors and gave us time to reflect on our goals for the year ahead, then find images to cut out from those magazines to match.

For anyone unfamiliar, a vision board is a visual representation of your goals. You can include images, affirmations, meaningful objects like shells or hearts, anything that stirs a sense of purpose, joy or direction. It's more than decoration. It cultivates positive expectancy, the sense that good things are on their way.

At that workshop, I found a picture of a cornucopia, a horn of plenty, overflowing with abundance. It symbolised financial wellbeing, joyful experiences, travel, love, and health. The image made me feel hopeful and excited. It still does.

Creating a vision board is not only effective, it's also fun. The collage of symbols and words becomes a daily visual reminder of what I'm moving toward. My current board includes pictures, affirmations, and powerful phrases like "Best Year Ever." That one's timeless. Every year can be better than the last.

I spoke with a few friends, successful ones, and was pleasantly surprised by how many of them create vision boards too. One even photographs theirs and makes it the lock screen on their phone.

I also like to choose a theme word for the year.

- When I first left corporate life, my word was *flow*.

- The next year was a little more dynamic, *momentum*.

- Then came *lift-off*. I filled my board with images of planes taking off. And, yes, my business took off that year.

Vision boards work because they help anchor your attention. They turn dreams into goals, and goals into intentions. They are visual cues that reinforce your certainty.

And certainty is key.

Another great tool for cultivating certainty? A bucket list. Write it down. Claim the experiences you want before you kick the bucket.

Because when you're clear on what you want, and ask for it daily, it's amazing what starts to show up.

Episode 160:
Dream Big with a Bucket List

Trav Bell

Tick It Before You Kick It:
Reclaiming Your Life Through a Bucket List

Before the world coined the phrase bucket list, Trav Bell was already living it. At just 18, he scribbled down a list of things to do before he died. No fanfare, just instinct. Something inside him knew that life wasn't meant to be lived on autopilot.

What started as a handwritten to-do list became his compass. A reason to get out of bed. A reason to say yes or no in business. His first career was in personal training. He pioneered PT studios in Australia, scaling to a franchise model. But over time, the joy drained out. He loved the product but felt trapped in a world of admin and legal contracts. He'd built himself a very tidy cage.

So he did what most don't; he walked away.

He leaned into coaching, NLP, and positive psychology. Then, at a speaking gig, a participant said, "You're like ... the bucket list guy." The name stuck. Trav rebranded. He didn't just run seminars; he built a movement. A global one.

His mission? To help 10 million people live purposely fulfilled lives before they die, or as he cheekily puts it, *"Tick it before you kick it."*

But here's what makes Trav's work so compelling. He's not just telling people to go skydiving or ride camels in Morocco. He's reframing what a bucket list really is. It's not just travel. It's not just thrill-seeking. It's about designing a life with intention.

He created an acronym – the MY BUCKETLIST Blueprint – designed to stretch the brain in all directions. The idea is to help people explore experiences across different areas of life: mental, spiritual, physical, emotional. It's a structured yet personal way to write a life plan.

Because that's what a bucket list is. A life plan in disguise.

Trav makes a strong case that your career plan should fit into your life plan, not the other way around. He says, *"Is it live to work? Or work to live?"* He wants people to stop waiting for retirement to live fully. To build a business or career that supports the life you want, not one that devours it.

And if you think this philosophy is only for individuals, think again. Trav's worked with leadership teams and C-Suite execs around the world. His message resonates just as deeply in boardrooms as it does in backyard BBQs.

Here's why: engagement.

Trav shared a scary stat. In Australia, roughly 70% of employees are disengaged at work. In the U.S., that number rises to 89%. That means 7 to 9 out of 10 people show up each day just going through the motions.

So he reframes the conversation. He says, *"You want better engagement at work? Help your people design their life outside of work."* A personal bucket list injects meaning back into the mundane. When people are excited about life, they bring that energy to work. They show up differently.

And for leaders? *"Put your own oxygen mask on first,"* he says. Lead by example. Be the kind of person others want to follow – vital, curious, optimistic, a person with a sense of adventure, a person who's not just surviving but living.

There's also the reverse bucket list, an exercise in gratitude. Write down what you've already achieved. You'll be amazed how many dreams you've quietly ticked off. We often forget. We focus so much on the next thing that we rarely pause to acknowledge how far we've come.

And when it comes to writing down your goals? Go analogue. Use a pen and paper. Neuroscience tells us the act of handwriting activates the brain differently. It embeds desire into your subconscious. Your reticular activating system (RAS) starts scanning the world for opportunities to fulfill those goals, even when you're not consciously looking.

Trav has over 350 items on his list. And he's still adding more.

As he says, *"Be curiously excited about the bigger version of yourself that exists on the other side of your bucket list."*

Because that's the point. The list isn't just about ticking boxes. It's about growth. It's about who you become in pursuit of the things that set your soul on fire.

Episode 141:
Asking is the Answer

Mark Victor Hansen
Crystal Dwyer Hansen

Asking Big, Thinking Bigger

When you sell over 90 million books, you've earned the right to call yourself the Ambassador of Possibility. But Mark Victor Hansen's secret isn't just catchy titles or good luck. It's the art of the *Ask*. This is no woo-woo manifesto. It's brass tacks motivation wrapped in stories about sleeping on floors, facing 144 rejections, and still betting big on a book about chicken soup and the soul.

In this unfiltered conversation, we travel from bankruptcy to bestsellers, from a kid buying his own clothes to building global empires, and always asking the next question.

Whether quoting the Bible, dropping Seth Godin anecdotes, or outlining the 7 roadblocks to asking, Mark doesn't just inspire, he challenges you to step up.

If you've ever doubted your worth, feared rejection, or waited too long to send the email that might change everything, this one's your wake-up call.

Spoiler alert: your dream life is just one bold ask away.

Which brings us to the ask.

Mark Victor Hansen, co-author of Chicken Soup for the Soul and more recently Ask! The Bridge from Your Dreams to Your Destiny, built an empire on the power of intentional, purposeful asking. His message? You don't need to have it all figured out. You just need to start asking better questions. Of yourself. Of others.

And, if you're spiritually inclined, of something greater than yourself.

> *Asking is the bridge. It's how you get from*
> *where you are to where you want to be.*
> —Mark Victor Hansen

Whether you're writing your first vision board, confronting doubts about worthiness or navigating a leadership role that demands clarity and courage, Mark's message lands. You're only one bold ask away from your next breakthrough.

Whether you're writing your first vision board, confronting doubts about worthiness, or navigating a leadership role that demands clarity and courage, Mark's message lands: you're only one bold ask away from your next breakthrough.

> *I ask for great plans for my future.*
> *I ask to discover my destiny.*
> *I ask for the fulfillment of my life purpose.*

Ask wisely. Ask prayerfully.

Ask with the quiet conviction that what you seek is already seeking you.

Throughout this chapter, we saw how motivation thrives on certainty, optimism, clear goals, and courageous action. By embracing tools like vision boards and bucket lists, and daring to ask boldly – as Mark Victor Hansen reminds us – you create momentum that sustains lasting motivation.

> Now it's your turn.
> Harness optimism.
> Cultivate clarity.
> Visualize boldly.
> Ask courageously.

EPILOGUE:
THE COURAGE TO ASK

If you made it this far, then something inside you is already shifting.

You explored frameworks, read insights from brilliant minds, and gathered strategies to lead with more intention.

But this final step, the act of asking, isn't just a nice-to-have. It's essential. Because asking isn't weakness; it's clarity, it's courage, it's leadership in motion.

The best leaders are Chief Motivation Officers, not just for their teams, but also for themselves. And motivation is a dance between belief and behavior. First you ask, then you act as if.

I've asked. I've been afraid to ask. I've asked boldly and been told no. And I've asked again. That's the path. That's the work. That's the privilege.

So now it's your turn.

Ask for what lights you up.
Ask for what scares you.
Ask for what moves you closer to your destiny.
And then, do.

Because your team is watching.
But more importantly, your future self is waiting.

Episode 89:
Nina's Career Story

Nina Sunday
Russell Pearson

Lifelong Reinventor

Russell Pearson introduces the conversation by calling me a lifelong reinventor. I accept the moniker. Not because I follow a carefully laid plan, but because I listen to that quiet inner voice, the one whispering, *"This chapter of your life is done. Let's write a new one."*

At university, I'm 19, already teaching speed reading. My uncle spots an opportunity when an American company lands in Brisbane, running TV ads. At his nudge, I take the course, hit 2,000 words per minute with excellent comprehension, and soon, I'm training others for the company. Accidental launch of a career in adult learning.

Early on, I realised something powerful. Learning fast means creating the ability to do almost anything. Speed reading is a superpower.

From Film School to Facilitation

After a year of high school teaching in Queensland, I answer the call to adventure and move to Sydney. What follows is a portfolio life: casual teaching, community theatre, bluegrass fiddle (self-taught, after years of classical violin exams and practising 3 lunch times a week in the school orchestra), then back to Queensland, to play fiddle in a country band. Won best instrumentalist in the Battle of the Bands.

To fund expensive sound gear, I discover a talent for selling: French wine, cinema ads, stainless steel cookware – direct sales. Because I create rapport easily with people, I'm successful at sales. Creativity stays alive through hobby courses in filmmaking.

The hobby becomes serious. I win a place at the Australian Film TV and Radio School's elite 3-year program.

After graduation, I land a dream job at ABC Television. But adult education keeps calling. I leap.

Building from Scratch

I project-manage international conferences. Build training products from scratch. Ideas scribbled on napkins turn into multi-city rollouts. I experiment. Sometimes nail it. Sometimes bomb. But I keep building.

What holds it all together isn't just curiosity; it's intentionality. I write a detailed description of my perfect career. It's the Mark Victor Hansen approach: ask for what you want ... great team, travel, awards, fun.

Every step, even the off-ramps, adds something new to the toolkit.

Building a Business with Scale and Soul

In 2001, I launch Brainpower Training, not just to teach speed reading and productivity, but to build a national business that scales without losing its soul. It evolves into a network of facilitators across 4 Australian cities.

Along the way, I introduce 30-day online challenges, start a globally streamed podcast (*Manage Self, Lead Others*), and build a speaking business that opens doors. I'm not in it for vanity metrics. I'm here to make work more human, one leader at a time.

Hard-Won Lessons

Here's what no one tells you when starting a business: talent alone won't cut it. You need structure, systems and feedback loops.

Early on, I bring someone onto the team and expect them to just figure it out. No roadmap, no conversation about what lights them up or drags them down. No one ever asked me those things either.

Eventually, I learn to ask, *"What are your strengths? What energises you? What drains you?"*

We swap tasks. Morale lifts. Retention follows.

The Sigmoid Curve: Know when to Re-motivate

Charles Handy's Sigmoid Curve changes how I think – about business, about people. What rises will fall ... unless you start a new curve while still on the first ascent. Applies to individuals, teams, products, motivation.

Change before you have to.

When team members plateau, it's not a title they need. It's growth. A fresh challenge. Something new to master. Re-motivating before the dip.

What Stays True

Through it all, I stay close to my centre: curiosity, the joy of discovery, reverence for communication, and a fascination with helping people work better together.

I create eLearning that runs on autopilot. Partner with an angel investor. Mentor interns, who go on to work in policy, medicine, global firms.

I don't wait for permission. I keep designing a life that evolves with intention.

My only regret? Not learning sooner how to bring others with me. Culture isn't decreed; it's co-created.

And leadership isn't sprinting ahead; it's ensuring no one's left behind. Eliyahu Goldratt said it best – the group can only go as fast as its slowest walker.

That's the real reinvention; growing others while growing yourself.

Episode 162:
Are We Losing Our
Deep Reading Brain?

Nina Sunday

Postscript:
Read Like Your Brain Depends On It

There's a slow burn happening. A silent book-burning. Not with fire, but with forgetting.

Ask someone if they read a book in the last year. One in 4 will say no. And that's not just a stat; that's a symptom.

Bookshops are vanishing. Publishers are hanging on by a thread. And people? People are reading headlines, not arguments. Tweets, not treatises. The dopamine's cheap and instant. And the cost? Our thinking.

I've seen it coming. Two decades teaching speed reading and I've watched the deep reading brain become an endangered species. We scroll, swipe, skim. But sit with a book? Rare.

Endure an idea from first page to last? Rarer still.

And that's the thing, books don't just feed knowledge. They sharpen cognition. They stretch focus. They unstick us from the shallow end of thought.

In preliterate societies, people think in anecdotes and immediacy. *"I've never seen a white bear, so I don't believe in them."* It's not stupidity, it's wiring. Reading rewires us. Literally.

It makes abstract thinking possible. Big-picture, critical, empathetic thinking. And now that wiring is getting frayed.

Neuroplasticity is real. What we do daily shapes our brains. If all we consume is clickbait and reels, guess what our thoughts start to sound like? Simple, slogany, black-and-white.

Like Orwell's sheep in *Animal Farm*: *"4 legs good, 2 legs bad."* That's where we're heading if we let books slip through our fingers.

So here's the call; not a polite one, but a guttural one ...

Drop everything and read.

Start with 10 minutes. A day. A week. A Friday afternoon. Make it sacred.

Try slow reading; not to study, not to conquer, but like meditation. Like it matters.

Get your hands on book summaries, sure. They're great previews. But don't stop there. Let them lure you into the full ride.

And if the idea of reading cover to cover terrifies you? Fine. Read at the speed of thought. Skim, scan, riff ... just stay with the flow.

Read fiction to grow empathy. Read nonfiction to grow clarity. Read because the world is complex and your brain deserves better than soundbites.

Read to keep your brain from fossilizing.

Because being well-read isn't about elitism. It's about survival. It's about staying sharp in a world that's slowly turning blunt.

And done is better than perfect.

So read. However you can. Just don't stop.

—Nina

REFERENCES

Nina Sunday, Brendan Rogers   podcast.thecultureofleadership.com

CONSTRUCTIVE CONVERSATIONS

Scott Dutton	fightingfair.com.au
Lisa McInnes-Smith	lisaspeaks.com
Andrew Bryant	selfleadership.com
Dan Silberberg	entelechy.ai/contact
Bruce Sullivan	brucesullivan.com
Natasha Hawker	employeematters.com.au
Rowdy Mclean	rowdymclean.com
Anneli Blundell	anneliblundell.com
Chris Dyer	chrisdyer.com
David Deane-Spread	metattude.com/resources
Carol Marzouk	leadershipnsoul.com
Brian Bowman	linkedin.com/in/brianbowman2
Val Grubb	valgrubbandassociates.com

FEEDBACK

Tricia Benn	heroceoclub.com
	c-suitenetwork.com
Corey Jones	prismwork.com
Mel Kettle	melkettle.com
Stacey Hanke	staceyhankeinc.com/connect
Fiona Robertson	fionarobertson.com

SELF-LEADERSHIP

Lynell Green	lynellsplace.com
Dan Silberberg	entelechy.ai/contact
Andrew Bryant	selfleadership.com
Onno Koelman	dynamicleaderdev.com

Bob Pizzini	robertpizzini.com/scheduled-events
Ian Stephens	ianstephensspeaks.com/contact-ian-stephens
Josh Levine	greatmondays.com

CULTURE

Jeffrey Hayzlett	c-suitenetwork.com
UKG	greatplacetowork.com/solutions/certification
Rachael Robertson	rachaelrobertson.com.au
Steve Simpson	steve-simpson.com
Gabrielle Dolan	gabrielledolan.com
Michael McQueen	michaelmcqueen.net

STRATEGY AND EXECUTION

Jim Gitney	strategyrealized.com
Martin Gonzalez	bonfiremoment.com
Jennifer Eggers	leadershiftinsights.com
Rod Collins	rodcollins.net
Nina Sunday	ninasunday.com
	brainpowertraining.com.au/signature-programs
Evan Hackel	dev.trainingunleashed.net

PSYCHOLOGICAL SAFETY

Nina Sunday	ninasunday.com
	brainpowertraining.com.au/signature-programs
Stephan Wiedner	noomii.com
	skillsetter.com
Leanne Faraday-Brash	brashconsulting.com.au
Paul Vittles	vittles.org

INFLUENCE

Dr Helen Turnbull	humanfacets.com
Linda Fisk	leadhershipglobal.com
Allan Parker	peakpd.com
Tim David	TimDavidSpeaks.com
Avish Parashar	avishparashar.com

APPRECIATION

Avi Liran	aviliran.com
Sheryl Lynn	joyely.com
Shivani Gupta	askshivani.com

PERSONAL BRANDING

Pamela Wigglesworth	experiential.sg
Yamini Naidu	yamininaidu.com.au

MOTIVATION

Helle Bundgaard	motivationfactor.com
Trav Bell	thebucketlistguy.com
Mark Victor Hansen	markvictorhansen.com

EPILOGUE

Russell Pearson	russellpearson.com
	russellpearson.com/marketing-podcast
Nina Sunday	ninasunday.com
	brainpowertraining.com.au/signature-programs

BIBLIOGRAPHY

PREFACE

1. Turing, A. M. (1952). "The chemical basis of morphogenesis." *Philosophical Transactions of the Royal Society of London. Series B, Biological Sciences*, 237(641), 37–72. https://doi.org/10.1098/rstb.1952.0012

INTRODUCTION

1. Garvin, D. A., Wagonfeld, A. B., & Kind, L. (2013, April). *Google's Project Oxygen: Do Managers Matter?* Harvard Business School Case 313-110 (Revised October 2013).

2. Goldratt, E. M., & Goldratt-Ashlag, E. (2010). *The Choice (Rev. ed.).* North River Press.

CONSTRUCTIVE CONVERSATIONS

1. Bryant, A. (2022). *The New Leadership Playbook: Being Human Whilst Successfully Delivering Accelerated Results.* Ocean Reeve Publishing.

2. Hawker, N. (2015). *From Hire to Fire and Everything in Between.* Natasha Hawker.

3. McLean, R. (2017). *Leadability.* Play Bigger Publishing

4. Armour, C., Blundell, A, & Cohen, B. (2015). *Developing Direct Reports: Taking The Guesswork Out of Leading Leaders.* Melbourne Bacca House Press.

5. Dyer, C. (2018). *The Power of Company Culture: How Any Business Can Build a Culture That Improves Productivity, Performance and Profits.* Koganpage.

6. Marzouk, C. (2025). *Taming Corporate Beasts: The Executive Lion Tamer's® Secrets to Mastering Big Egos and Difficult Leaders.*

7. Grubb, V. M. (2017). *Clash Of the Generations: Managing the New Workplace Reality.* Wiley.

FEEDBACK

1. Stromberg, L., Nichols, J., & Jones, C. (2023). *Intentional Power: The 6 Essential Leadership Skills for Triple Bottom Line Impact.* Wiley.

2. Kettle, M. (2022). *Fully Connected: How Great Leaders Prioritise Themselves, Reclaim Their Energy and Find Joy.* BookPOD.

3. Brown, B. (2018). *Dare to lead: Brave work. Tough conversations. Whole hearts.* Random House.

4. Hanke, S. (2024). *Influence Elevated: Maximizing Your Connection Monday to Monday.* Stacey Hanke Inc.

5. Robertson, F. (2022). *Rules of Belonging: Change Your Organisational Culture, Delight Your People and Turbo Charge Your Results.* Major Street Publishing.

SELF LEADERSHIP

1. Kegan, R, Laskow Lahey, L. (2009). *Immunity to Change: How to Overcome It and Unlock the Potential in Yourself and Your Organization.* Harvard Business Review Press.

2. Merron, K. (2020). *The Art of Transformational Coaching: A Guidebook for Helping Others Heal and Transform.* Tonic Books.

3. Van der Kolk, B. A. (2014). *The Body Keeps the Score: Brain, Mind, And Body in The Healing of Trauma.*

4. Gordon, J. S. (2008). *Unstuck: Your guide to the seven-stage journey out of depression.* Penguin Press.

CULTURE

1. Hayzlett, J. (2018). *HERO FACTOR: How Great Leaders Transform Cultures and Create Winning Organizations.* Entrepreneur press.

2. McQueen, M. (2023). *Mindstuck: Mastering the Art of Changing Minds*. Dean Publishing.

3. Levine, J. (2018). *Great Mondays: How to Design a Company Culture Employees Love*. McGraw Hill.

4. Wiseman, L., & McKeown, G. (2010). *Multipliers: How the best leaders make everyone smarter*. HarperBusiness

5. Robertson, R. (2020). *Respect trumps harmony: Why Being Liked Is Overrated and Constructive Conflict Gets Results*. Wiley.

6. Simpson, S., & Stef Du Plessis. (2015). *A Culture Turned: Using UGRs to Boost Performance and Culture*. CreateSpace.

7. Dolan, G. (2021). *Magnetic Stories: Connect With Customers and Engage Employees with Brand Storytelling*. John Wiley & Sons Australia, Ltd.

STRATEGY AND EXECUTION

1. Gitney, J. (2023). *Strategy Realized – The Business Hierarchy of Needs®*. Jim Gitney.

2. Gonzalez, M., & Yellin, J. (2024). *The Bonfire Moment*. HarperCollins.

3. Eggers, J., & Barlow, C. (2019). *Resilience: It's Not About Bouncing Back: How Leaders and Organizations Can Build Resilience Before Disruption Hits*. Best Seller Publishing.

4. Collins, R. (2024). *Nobody Is Smarter Than Everybody: Why Self-Managed Teams Make Better Decisions and Deliver Extraordinary Results*. CLS Publishing.

PSYCHOLOGICAL SAFETY

1. Sunday, N. (2018). *Workplace Wisdom For 9 To Thrive: Proven Tactics and Hacks to Get Ahead in Today's Workplace*. Nina Sunday.

2. Faraday-Brash, L. (2012). *Vulture Cultures: How To Stop Them Ravaging Your Organisation's Performance, People, Profit and Public Image*. Australian Academic Press Group.

3. Edmondson, A. C. (1999). *Psychological safety and learning behavior in work teams. Administrative Science Quarterly, 44*(2), 350–383

4. Google LLC. (2015). *Project Aristotle* [Research study]. Google re:Work.

5. Ahmedani, B. K., Penfold, R. B., Boggs, J. M., Richards, J., Simon, G. E., et al. (2025). *Zero Suicide Model implementation and suicide attempt rates in outpatient mental health care. JAMA Network Open, 8*(4), e253721. https://doi.org/10.1001/jamanetworkopen.2025.3721

INFLUENCE

1. Turnbull, H. (2012). *Unconscious Bias – Blind Spots: An Interview on Unconscious Bias.* Hope of Vision Publishing.

2. Derksen, C., & Fisk, L. (2025). *LeadHERship Unveiled: Women Leading with Impact.* Action Takers Publishing.

3. David, T. (2015). *Magic Words: The Science and Secrets Behind Seven Words That Motivate, Engage, and Influence.* Prentice Hall Press.

4. Parashar, A. (2012). *Say "Yes, And!": 2 Little Words That Will Transform Your Career, Organization, and Life!.* Avish Parashar Productions, Inc.

APPRECIATION

1. Lee, D., & Liran, A. (2021). *First Time Leadership.* Ocean Reeve Publishing.

2. Nooyi, I. (2021). *My Life in Full: Work, Family, And Our Future.* Portfolio.

3. Conley, C. (2018). *Wisdom at work: The Making of a Modern Elder.* Crown Currency

4. Gupta, S. (2024). *Getting Your People to Step Up: 7 Simple Strategies to Attract and Keep Your Key Talent*. John Wiley & Sons.

5. Lynn, S., & Scottlin, A. (2023). *Chair of Joy*. Joyely.

PERSONAL BRANDING

1. Wigglesworth, P. (2014). *Public Relations: An Easy, Step-by-step Guide to Creating a Public Relations Plan (Small Business Marketing Mentor Book 1)*. Experiential Pte Ltd.

2. Naidu, Y. (2023). *X Factor: Unleash Your Presenting Superpower*. Yamini Naidu Consulting.

MOTIVATION

1. Seligman, M. E. P. (1991). *Learned optimism*. A. A. Knopf.

2. Vroom, V. H. (1964). *Work and motivation*. Wiley.

3. Bundgaard, H. (2014). *The Motivated Brain*. CreateSpace Independent Publishing Platform.

4. Mark Victor Hansen, and Crystal Dwyer Hansen. (2020). *Ask!: The Bridge from Your Dreams to Your Destiny*. Post Hill Press.

EPILOGUE

1. Handy, C. B. (1994). *The Empty Raincoat: Making Sense of the Future*. Hutchinson.

2. Goldratt, E. M., & Cox, J. (2004). *The Goal: A Process of Ongoing Improvement (3rd rev. ed., 20th anniversary ed.)*. North River Press

3. Orwell, G. (1945). *Animal Farm*. Secker & Warburg.

Join the
NINA SUNDAY
Podcast Club

If you made it this far, you're my kind of people. Here's your invitation to stay in the inner circle. Join me on my Substack channel: *The Nina Sunday Podcast Club.*

Think of it as our own space to access candid conversations with from my NotebookLM *Deep Dive* sessions where two sharp, AI co-hosts riff, question, and bounce around ideas sparked by the published podcast conversation.

It's like a morning-after review with sparks that fly when fresh ideas spill out with honesty, curiosity, and freedom to roam wherever a good conversation wants to go.

But this isn't just a broadcast; it's our community of forward-thinkers who know real culture is built through real talk and staying curious together.

Visit **ninasunday.substack.com** and pull up a chair. More good stuff happens when the On Air light is off; and this time, you're in the room.

Need a conference speaker or workshop or retreat facilitator who can shake things up in Australia-Pacific, USA, and worldwide, wherever your team needs it. Let's talk:

BrainpowerTraining.com.au | ninasunday.com

DISCLAIMER

The material included in this book is designed to provide information and practical tips for readers and give general guidance only. Advice in this book is derived from the author's research and professional experience. No warranties or guarantees are expressed or implied by the content in this book.

Material is compressed and simplified for educational purposes and should not create expectations about how you may deal with any specific matter in particular circumstances. The reader is responsible for their own choices, actions and results.

The publisher accepts no liability for loss or damage that may be suffered by any person or entity that relies on information in this book. The purpose of this book is to increase understanding and awareness of the topic. The material should be used fairly and accurately.

ABOUT THE AUTHOR

After starting my career as a high school teacher, I swapped chalk for filmmaking with 3 years studying at the *Australian Film, TV and Radio School (AFTRS)*. Landing a job at a national TV channel, I eventually realised the supposed dream job had no mentorship or real path forward.

So, I wrote my own story.

Drawing on years of teaching speed reading and a couple more developing my own improved method, I launched a corporate training company, Brainpower Training. It grew into a national network of facilitators sharing my people skills workshops across Australia.

After decades in Sydney I moved back to hometown Brisbane, until the pandemic suddenly hit pause on everything. That's when my podcast passion project took centre stage. I launched the *Manage Self, Lead Others* show, focusing on what it means to lead in uncertain times.

Along the way, I picked up certifications in Adult Learning, Prosci® Change Management, Design Thinking, NLP, Emotional Intelligence, DiSC® and earned CSP (Certified Speaking Professional) and CVP (Certified Virtual Presenter) designations. Having served as Chapter President for Professional Speakers Australia in both New South Wales and Queensland, I was honoured with a Speaker Hall of Fame Nevin award.

Need a conference speaker or workshop or retreat facilitator who can shake things up – Australia-Pacific, USA, and worldwide, wherever your team needs it? Let's talk:

BrainpowerTraining.com.au | ninasunday.com

www.ingramcontent.com/pod-product-compliance
Lightning Source LLC
Chambersburg PA
CBHW031954190326
41520CB00007B/241